Eyes Wide Open

Emotional purity is an issue that I, and many of my friends, face today. This book opened my eyes to the consequences of an unguarded heart and motivated me to act and think in a way that would be pleasing to God.

Kiersten, age 15
Bradenton, Florida

Who can know the heart and all of its deceitful desires? God, and only God. Brienne Murk recognizes this truth with passionate conviction in *Eyes Wide Open*. Her candidness allows young people like myself to relate to her experiences and identify areas of conviction in our own relationships and lives.

Jennifer Barringer, age 20
2006 NCAA First-Team All-American Distance Runner
University of Colorado, Boulder

There are a lot of good dating and purity books out there, but most of them are clearly aimed at one facet of relationships—finding the right person, choosing purity, why to be pure, or how to stay pure. Brienne Murk writes about the total package and provides a practical guide to living out purity in relationships.

Alyse Pritchard, age 23
Tacoma, Washington

In *Eyes Wide Open*, Brienne offers a fresh perspective regarding personal purity and its effects on those relationships.

Tim Arens, Ed.D.
Dean of Students, Moody Bible Institute
Chicago, Illinois

Eyes Wide Open is definitely an eye-opener. Brienne takes guarding your heart to a higher level and gives positive building blocks to lay the foundation for saving many future broken hearts. Where was this book when I was in high school?!

Shelly Ballestero
OnCourse magazine
CBN.com Beauty and Health Contributor and *Lifestyle* Beauty Editor

Brilliant. Purposeful. Brienne delivers a compelling message on how it is possible in an age of sensational mass media bombardment to live in complete purity in body, soul and spirit, following biblical principles through faith and obedience. *Eyes Wide Open* is a godly manual for Christian relationships.

Rev. Renee Branson
President/Director, Mountain Top Ministries, Inc.
Pastoral Care Minister, Lakewood Church, Houston, Texas

I am amazed by the honesty and impressed by the truth that Brienne brings to the table. *Eyes Wide Open* reminds us of the importance of emotional purity and of keeping our thoughts pointed toward an even greater tie.

Eva Marie Everson
Coauthor of *Sex, Lies and the Media* and *Sex, Lies and High School*

In *Eyes Wide Open*, Brienne offers guidance and wise advice to avoid common traps and live in emotional as well as physical purity before God and man. It is encouraging to see a young woman so devoted to purity who is reaching out to teenagers.

Ron Luce
President and Founder, Teen Mania Ministries

It is so refreshing to see a beautiful, talented young woman who marches to a different drummer. This book can change the hearts and moral standards of this needy generation of youth and serve as an important instrument for revival.

Shirley Rose
Author, Speaker, Executive Producer and Host of *Aspiring Women*

EYES WIDE OPEN

AVOIDING THE HEARTBREAK OF EMOTIONAL PROMISCUITY

BRIENNE MURK

Regal

From Gospel Light
Ventura, California, U.S.A.

Published by Regal Books
From Gospel Light
Ventura, California, U.S.A.
Printed in the U.S.A.

Regal Books is a ministry of Gospel Light, a Christian publisher dedicated to serving the local church. We believe God's vision for Gospel Light is to provide church leaders with biblical, user-friendly materials that will help them evangelize, disciple and minister to children, youth and families.

It is our prayer that this Regal book will help you discover biblical truth for your own life and help you meet the needs of others. May God richly bless you.

For a free catalog of resources from Regal Books/Gospel Light, please call your Christian supplier or contact us at 1-800-4-GOSPEL *or* www.regalbooks.com.

Library of Congress Cataloging-in-Publication Data
Murk, Brienne.
  Eyes wide open : avoiding the heartbreak of emotional promiscuity / Brienne Murk.
    p. cm.
  ISBN 978-0-8307-4492-3 (trade paper)
  1. Man-woman relationships—Religious aspects—Christianity. 2. Emotions—Religious aspects—Christianity. 3. Sex—Religious aspects—Christianity. 4. Conduct of life. I. Title.
  BT705.8.M87 2007
  248.4—dc22   2007007565

Rights for publishing this book in other languages are contracted by Gospel Light Worldwide, the international nonprofit ministry of Gospel Light. Gospel Light Worldwide also provides publishing and technical assistance to international publishers dedicated to producing Sunday School and Vacation Bible School curricula and books in the languages of the world. For additional information, visit www.gospellightworldwide.org; write to Gospel Light Worldwide, P.O. Box 3875, Ventura, CA 93006; or send an e-mail to info@gospellightworldwide.org.

To my future husband—
I loved you before I even knew you.

Contents

Foreword

Coming of age in the twenty-first century is not easy. Sexuality has become a battlefield where the forces of good and evil seek to capture the attention of youth. On the one hand is the contemporary secular view that sex is a biological need, like drinking water: You are thirsty, so you drink water. You have sexual urges, so you fulfill them whenever, wherever and with whomever. In short, sex is a form of recreation. On the other side is the Christian view that sex is God's idea and He has given us guidelines that require abstinence before marriage. Sex within marriage becomes the unique expression of our deep companionship and unites us in a lifelong loving relationship.

As a counselor for over 30 years, I have never met a man or woman who regretted following the biblical plan, but I have met thousands who are trying to find healing for the pain they have experienced because they have treated sex lightly. The young girls who have lost their virginity and the young men who took it from them both weep when they realize that they have been deceived.

A series of broken relationships is not the foundation for a good marriage. The best marriages are built upon a foundation of integrity, discipline, self-control and love.

and forth—sometimes more than 20 per day.

On Thanksgiving of my junior year in high school, Eric called and said he wanted to talk about Us. (I knew this was serious . . . I could hear the capital "U" in his voice.) As we talked, it became clear that his feelings ran much deeper than friendship.

I had to consider if I felt the same way. Eric knew I had a passion to minister to youth about the issue of purity, and during the course of our conversation he said that he felt a similar calling. Rather than being suspicious that he was telling me what he thought I wanted to hear, I took his words as a "sign from God" and let myself become even more emotionally attached.

After that conversation, our relationship took a subtle but irreversible turn. Eric and I started to be very open and vulnerable with each other. We talked about our hopes and dreams for the future. We talked about how long we thought an engagement should be, how many kids we wanted, what kind of careers we aspired to. These exchanges were mostly online, and because we rarely talked in person, we felt safe to pour out our hearts without the awkwardness of talking face to face.

Like it or not, we both had to live with the emotions that were awakened. Up to that point, there was a sort of invisible barrier in our relationship. We both had made a commitment to remain sexually pure until marriage and I had even taken that commitment one step further: When I turned sixteen, I believe God asked me not to date until I knew I had met the man I would marry, and I made a commitment to obey. You may think that's a bit extreme (and it is)—God certainly doesn't ask it of everyone, but I know it's what He called me to do.

I can't tell you how thankful I am that I made that promise, because it kept me from getting even more intensely involved with Eric. Even so, we were oblivious to the fact that our intimate conversations pushed against the boundary lines that we had established. I was blind to my inconsistency with the commitment I had made to guard my heart, and even though Eric had expressed a similar commitment, he wasn't a strong Christian and didn't have the best track record when it came to relationships. I didn't realize how his previous relationship patterns made it difficult for him to know how to guard his heart.

My life verse at that time was Proverbs 4:23, which says, "Guard your heart above all else, for it determines the course of your life." We both knew the timing wasn't right for us to begin a serious relationship, but we were having myself out of the picture," I told him, "and I think you need to seriously consider what's most important in your life—me or God."

I think part of me was putting Eric to a test. I wanted to see if he would still strive to be a man of God even if it wasn't for me. For a few months, it seemed he was doing just that, and I fantasized about the possibility of our being together one day. But soon enough, he slipped back into his old patterns, and by the middle of summer, he was dating another girl in our youth group.

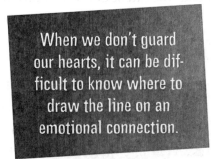

When we don't guard our hearts, it can be difficult to know where to draw the line on an emotional connection.

I was crushed—not so much because I still liked him, but because he had lied to me about his convictions and I had fallen for it. He told me what he thought I wanted to hear, and because I was so entrenched in my own emotions, I was unable to think clearly and evaluate his motives. I let my guard down and got burned. As I sobbed with regret, all I could think was, *How could I have been so wrong?!*

Although I hadn't crossed any lines sexually, I had allowed myself to fall into the trap of emotional promiscuity. I had ignored the boundaries I'd set for myself and learned the hard way that when we don't guard our hearts, it can be difficult to know where to draw the line on an emotional connection.

Purity of Heart

My story is not unique. Our culture propagates the false belief that nothing our hearts desire can harm us. As a result, many young men and women have struggled with the concept of purity and experienced the pain a broken heart can bring. Whether it's because of sexual promiscuity or emotional attachment, the sting and devastation accompanying a broken heart can seem unbearable.

How do we incorporate purity into our lives? Many enthusiastically join the "True Love Waits" movement, which focuses on sexual purity. You've no doubt read books or articles or watched videos about abstinence, so I'm not going to repeat the great advice you've already heard from people like Joshua Harris, Rebecca St. James, Josh McDowell, Lakita Garth and a host of others. However, with so much talk about abstinence, some people have inadvertently presumed that as long as we're not sexually active, we're living in purity—which just isn't the case. I think these authors would agree with me that merely practicing physical abstinence is not enough. Honoring God means more than sexual purity—it means purity of heart.

Maybe you've picked up this book because you're sick and tired of relationships that lead to pain and disappointment. Maybe you've given pieces of your heart away prematurely, only to be repaid with sorrow. Maybe you're in a relationship right now and you want to know how to stay focused on God and live in purity. Or maybe you just want to avoid the pain of a broken heart. Though I haven't found a magic cure for the broken-heart blues (yet!), I'd like to share some ideas that can make navigating the slippery slopes of relationships a lot less painful, a lot more satisfying and much more honoring to God.

Falling for a Fairy Tale

Wouldn't it be nice if everything turned out the way it does in fairy tales? The prince saves the princess, they overcome impossible obstacles to fall in love and then they live happily ever after. Isn't that what's supposed to happen? Fairy tales lead us to fantasize about the perfect kiss in the perfect setting with the perfect person (like Mia's search for a "foot poppin'" kiss in *The Princess Diaries*), and we've started to believe that the Hollywood version of romance is the only way to go.

On top of that, our emotions are greatly influenced by social expectations, and little by little, our sense of propriety and purity is being eroded by our culture. Our view of what is "appropriate" is being overrun by a barrage of enticing and sexually explicit images. How are we as young people who want to honor God supposed to stand up against the pressure to conform?

Everywhere we turn, billboards, magazines, music and store window displays bombard us with sexuality. Clothing lines like Guess?, Abercrombie & Fitch and Victoria's Secret tell us to flaunt it if we've got it. We can't turn on the TV without seeing a big-busted blonde trying to sell us shampoo or toilet bowl cleaner, or a couple hooking up because of microwave popcorn or antiperspirant.

Magazines like *Cosmopolitan, Teen People* and *Seventeen* fill our minds with pictures of the "perfect" body, hair, makeup and clothes. And with articles ranging from "Top Ten Hottest Hunks" to "999 Ways to Look Sexy," from "What He's Thinking While You're Making Out" to "Ten Ways to Improve Your Sex Life," is it any wonder that we think relationships are about sex? Is it any wonder that we find ourselves looking for love in physical relationships?

Movies are filled with graphic scenes of stars jumping into bed with each other in wild, onscreen "romances," and these portrayals of extramarital affairs and explicit sex have perverted romance into something for sexual gratification and personal benefit.

In previous generations, musicians sang about a longing for peace and the innocence of young love. Today, female pop stars lock lips on international television while others bare all for the camera. Other "artists" get top billing by openly mocking the lifestyle of purity and those who choose it.

In the fifties, popular television shows like *I Love Lucy* and *Leave It to Beaver* celebrated an ideal of the happy, healthy family in a comedic and innocent way. Today, TV shows celebrate the exploits of people trying to get laid. Shows like *Talk Soup* fill our minds with useless gossip, tantalizing us with stories of celebrity flings or rumors of infidelity. Reality shows like *Extreme Makeover* are devoted to dieting, training, nipping, suctioning and tucking people into the "perfect body." On soaps like *Desperate Housewives* or *The O.C.,* the whole story is about who's dating whom, who's breaking up with whom and who's sleeping with whom.

> Unlike the movies, most relationships don't have fairytale endings.

I'm sure you never watched the reality TV series *The Bachelorette,* but . . . I admit I watched it. I wanted to see what had everybody talking! As the field of hopeful guys narrowed from 25 to 15 to 8 to 4 and finally down to 2 remaining men, I was on pins and needles.

Each time the Bachelorette had to choose who to send home and who to keep for another week, she said something like "I'm gonna go with my gut" or "I'm letting my heart decide." On the last episode, she told Guy #1 that from the first night she saw him she felt drawn to him, that they really had a connection and that every moment they'd spent together since had confirmed her attraction.

"But," she said, "my heart has led me in another direction."

Isn't that what our culture tells us? *Follow your heart. If it feels right, it* is *right.* Even Disney movies teach us that *true love conquers all.* But unlike the movies, most relationships don't have fairytale endings and "love's first kiss" is rarely saved for Prince Charming. Instead of holding out for God's best, most of us look for love in all the wrong places and end up with a broken heart and a lot of excess emotional baggage.

The band Superchic[k] has a great song called "Princes and Frogs." My favorite line asks what Prince Charming would think if he came riding into your life when you're kissing a frog. Now that's an image that sticks in my mind! I would much rather spend my time living for God and preparing myself for my future spouse than kissing a long line of slimy reptiles that eat bugs.

Relationships: More than Romance

There is a lot more to relationships than romance. The Bible is full of passages that tell us to love one another, but we can't stop there—we must dig deeper to find out *how* to love one another. Scripture talks about three different kinds of male-female relationships: *blood relative* (parent, sibling, aunt, uncle, cousin, and so on), *marriage* and *friendship*. Did you notice that *romantic relationship* is never mentioned outside of marriage? Now I'm not saying it's wrong to be romantically involved with someone—it's a different world than Bible times and we don't arrange marriages nowadays, either! Let's be honest, though: Times change, but people and God's standards don't. The Bible is still our best measuring stick for how the human heart should line up with God's heart, and according to the Bible, a truly pure relationship is based on more than just romance.

The Bible reveals a higher standard for relationships than our culture's standard. Paul tells us in Romans 12:10 to "love each other with genuine affection and take delight in honoring each other." I can't think of a better example of this verse than my friend Jake.

> The Bible reveals a higher standard for relationships than our culture's standard.

Jake grew up in a non-Christian home and was abused as a child. Because he never experienced the love he needed, he spent his teenage years looking for love and acceptance in all the wrong places. He got involved with the occult and participated in pagan religious ceremonies.

I met Jake when he was in his early 20s and invited him to church. Within a month, he accepted Jesus as his Savior and started growing by leaps and bounds. Less than two years later, he started taking correspondence courses from a Bible school with plans to become a missionary.

I've never seen anyone with a better understanding of what it means to love people with genuine affection. Jake truly delights in serving people. He's the first person to volunteer for thankless jobs and the last person to leave when something needs to be done. He treats my sister and me as younger sisters in the Lord and has never even tried to take advantage of our friendship.

Even though he's only been a Christian for three years, Jake sets an amazing example of what the Bible says in 1 Peter 1:22: "You were cleansed from your sins when you obeyed the truth, so now you must show sincere love to each other as brothers and sisters. Love each other deeply with all your heart." The apostle Peter elaborated on how to do this in his second letter:

In view of all this, make every effort to respond to God's promises. Supplement your faith with a generous provision of moral excellence, and moral excellence with knowledge, and knowledge with self-control, and self-control with patient endurance, and patient endurance with godliness, and godliness with brotherly affection, and brotherly affection with love for everyone (2 Pet. 1:5-7).

If we start with faith as our foundation and build relationships from there, we see that moral excellence, knowledge, self-control, patience, endurance and godliness are all necessary if we want God-honoring relationships that run deeper than mere romance.

The way we conduct our relationships is also important. In Paul's first letter to Timothy, he tells him to "talk to younger men as you would to your own brothers. Treat older women as you would your mother, and treat younger women with all purity as you would your own sisters" (5:2). We are to treat everyone as a brother or sister in the Lord. That means taking time to help people out by serving at church, taking a meal to someone in need, or volunteering to help in the nursery—regardless of what we get out of it. We do it out of pure love.

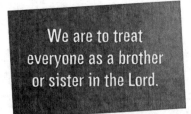

We are to treat everyone as a brother or sister in the Lord.

If we are going to treat everyone with brotherly or sisterly affection, we must learn to view everyone equally . . . which is a lot easier said than done. It's easy to respect or want to impress someone who's cute or has a nice body— it's another thing to affectionately care for someone who is not very attractive or is considered a social outcast! But God created each one of us in His image, and every person is worthy of respect, honor and affection—regardless of whether or not we meet the world's standards of beauty, talent or intellect. If we catch ourselves treating certain people better than others, it's probably a good time to do a heart check and reevaluate our motives.

In order to live up to God's standard for loving relationships, we need a radical change in our thought patterns when it comes to relating to and interacting with members of the opposite sex. At one of the first seminars I taught on this subject, one of the guys asked, "If I treat all girls like someone special, won't they get the wrong idea and think I'm interested in them?" I told him that the key is to develop a reputation for treating *everyone* with honor and respect, regardless of who they are or what they look like. If your motives are pure and you treat all people with the same affection and esteem, people will realize that you are someone who can be trusted.

Non-romantic, opposite-sex relationships are a foreign concept in our culture. We tend to look at all male-female relationships as romantic or sexual, but it doesn't have to be this way. According to God's Word, it *shouldn't* be this way! We need to consider whether or not we are honoring someone when we judge a relationship based on what we can get out of it, or begin relationships wondering "Is this the one?" If our desire is to honor God, we need to focus on loving each other as brothers and sisters in the Lord rather than trying to find a boyfriend or girlfriend.

What Is True Love?

Love can be defined in many ways. Love is tender affection for another person, such as the love Jesus tells us to have for our Christian brothers and sisters. Love is a feeling of warm personal attachment or deep fondness, such as the kind of love felt for a parent, child or friend. Love is sexual passion or desire, a feeling often confused with lust. Love is the person toward whom love is felt ("my love"), such as a boyfriend or girlfriend. Love is kind concern for the well-being of others, which motivates us to check up on a sick friend or an ailing grandparent. And finally, love is the generous affection God has for His creation.

Did you notice that only two of those definitions have to do with romantic feelings or sexual desires? Most of the descriptions are related to "tender affection," which is a far cry from the fiery lust we so often associate with the word "love." When the Bible presents God's view of romantic love, it looks quite different from what we've gotten used to. The writer of Song of Solomon, for instance, referred to his bride as "my sister" (see Song of Solomon 4–5). Before you get too grossed out, the writer didn't mean "sister" like *sister*. "Sister" was a Hebrew term of endearment that meant the writer intended to love and protect his wife as he would love and protect his sister, with honor and purity.

God is the inventor of romance, and He intends that even relationships bursting with passion and desire are grounded in respect and affection. His instructions for us are clearly laid out in the world's greatest love letter (that is, the Bible), which says:

> Love is patient and kind. Love is not jealous or boastful or proud or rude. It does not demand its own way. It is not irritable, and it keeps no record of being wronged. It does not rejoice about injustice but rejoices whenever the truth wins out. Love never gives up, never loses faith, is always hopeful, and endures through every circumstance (1 Cor. 13:4-7).

The biblical definition of love stands in such stark contrast to the typical Hollywood romance. The enticing and exciting love the world offers is just a feeble counterfeit of the deep and powerful romance that God created, yet we have blurred the line between reality and fantasy so much that we can no longer tell the difference between the real thing and a cheap knock-off.

> The enticing and exciting love the world offers is just a feeble counterfeit of the deep and powerful romance that God created.

Proverbs 15:26 says that "the LORD detests evil plans, but he delights in pure words." Each of us has a God-shaped hole in our lives that nothing else can fill, but many of us try to stuff it full of the plastic beauty, phony perfection and bogus intimacy that the world offers. Bit by bit, we allow the world to steal our hearts away rather than waiting for the only person—Jesus Christ—who can bring us satisfaction, fulfillment and true love.

Purity: It's Not Just About Sex

As Christians, we are set apart for God's purpose and are called to live by God's standards. The sexual purity movement is an attempt to honor God's standard for opposite-sex relationships. While I applaud the efforts of writers and speakers who address the sexual aspect of purity, I fear they stop short of defining what true purity is. As a result, many Christian young people are making commitments to physical abstinence while practicing emotional promiscuity.

We generally associate the terms "purity" and "promiscuity" with sex, but in reality they are much broader terms. Wikipedia defines "promiscuity" as "the practice of making relatively casual and indiscriminate choices."[1] Isn't this exactly how we behave in most dating relationships? Even if we aren't having sex, endless cycles of dating and breaking up are, by definition, *promiscuous*. We are casually and indiscriminately giving away our hearts, one piece at a time.

"Purity," on the other hand, is defined as: (1) being free from contamination; (2) freedom from admixture (alien

elements or ingredients); (3) ceremonial or ritual clean-
ness; (4) freedom from guilt or evil; innocence; or (5) physical chastity, virginity.[2] I find it significant that the primary
definitions of "purity" have absolutely nothing whatsoever
to do with sex! Purity has to do with innocence and freedom from guilt or contamination.

> True purity is not
> connected merely to our
> sexuality, but to every
> part of our lives.

Like so many others, I used to think that purity was
about sex. I thought that if I stayed a virgin until I got
married, I'd be pure. In the last few years, however, I've
realized that true purity is not connected merely to our
sexuality, but to every part of our lives. Purity has to do
with movies we watch, books we read, clothes we wear,
friends we hang out with, words we say, places we go, people we date and things we do. Purity has to do with how
we think, what we nurture inside our hearts and how we
express our passions and desires. Purity has to do with

refusing to give our hearts to people who aren't worthy to be entrusted with such a precious gift, and instead waiting for the man or woman who will spend his or her entire life cherishing us with godly, tender affection.

Too often we equate purity with virginity. While virginity is obviously an important element of purity, not every guy or girl who is a virgin lives a pure lifestyle. And just because a guy or girl is no longer a virgin doesn't mean he or she can never live a life of purity.

(If you're reading this book and you've already lost your virginity, don't allow Satan to keep you in bondage to guilt. Whether you gave away your virginity willingly or it was taken from you by force, God is a God of second chances! No matter what your past may be, He wants you to live in purity from this day forward. In order to do that, you need to recognize the areas in your life where impurity continues to exist and turn away from it. You *can* honor God in your relationships, starting today!)

As a whole, our society is empty of purity and it can be a struggle to find a biblical definition of purity. (And once we find it, it can be difficult to learn how to live out our commitment in a practical way!) The first key to living in purity is to recognize the areas in our lives that are impure—only after we recognize the impurity can we confess it to God and turn away (that is, repent) from it.

Guarding Your Heart

Regardless of your past, purity begins with your heart. God is not as concerned with outward things as He is with what your heart looks like. Don't get me wrong—I'm not saying that God doesn't care about things like modesty and make-out sessions! God says to be holy because He is holy (see 1 Pet. 1:16), so we should always exercise self-control. But we are deceiving ourselves if we define purity by our outward actions. Whether we're dating, courting or "just friends," it's essential that we realize that avoidance of sexual involvement doesn't guarantee a pure heart.

Purity begins with your heart.

First Samuel 16:7 says, "The LORD doesn't see things the way you see them. People judge by outward appearance, but the LORD looks at the heart." In Luke 6:45, Jesus said, "A good person produces good things from the treasury of a good heart, and an evil person produces evil things from the treasury of an evil heart. What you say flows from what is in your heart." Everything we think, do and say is dependent on our heart's condition—that's why it's so critical that we guard it!

Practicing sexual abstinence while engaging in premature emotional intimacy is not true purity. When we fall into the trap of thinking that it is, we begin the process of becoming ensnared by emotional promiscuity. We fail to realize how easy (and dangerous) it is to give our hearts away long before we give our bodies.

Pushing the Limits

If you've been a Christian for any length of time, you have no doubt experienced the sorrow and emptiness that result from breaking God's laws. One of my favorite authors is Frank Peretti, who describes sin (impurity) as "a burning sore around the heart."[3] At first you may not notice it, but after a while it begins to ache, then burn, until finally the pain is so intense that there is nowhere you can run to get away from it.

I've met scores of people who have messed up in the area of sexual purity and suffered disastrous consequences. Every single one has told me that their failure came because they started pushing the line, ignoring the twinges of guilt and discomfort until it got easier and easier to rationalize their behavior. Before they knew it, their heart was rubbed raw and bleeding. I know countless girls who thought that having sex with their boyfriends would draw them closer together and cement their relationship, but it only drove a wedge between them—often destroying the friendship they once had. The pain of dishonoring God and losing their relationship was almost too much to bear.

> True purity is not trying to see how close we can get to the line, but seeing how close we can get to God.

As humans, it's natural to want to test the limits, but when we start to think "How far is too far?" we've already lit the fire of impurity in our hearts. Somehow we've been persuaded that as long as we don't score, we're okay—but 1 Corinthians 6:12-13 says:

Everything is permissible, but not everything is beneficial. The body is not meant for sexual immorality, but for the Lord, and the Lord for the body (*NIV*).

Just because we're not going "all the way" doesn't mean our actions or thoughts are pure. True purity is not trying to see how close we can get to the line, but seeing how close we can get to God.

Living in Purity

While it's true that right actions don't guarantee purity, a pure heart expresses itself in right actions. So what about you? Do the movies you watch, friends you hang out with, words you say and places you go show people that you are committed to living in purity? It might sound like a cheap cliché, but actions really do speak louder than words. Jesus said, "You can identify them by their fruit, that is, by the way they act" (Matt. 7:16). Does the "fruit" in your life identify you as pure, or does it leave people wondering about the depth of your convictions? To ask it another way, does your lifestyle show that God is number one in your life, or is He taking a backseat to your sexual desires and emotional fantasies?

How often do we compromise on the books we read or movies and TV shows we watch because "there's just a little bit of impurity" in them? I mean, what's a five-minute sex scene in a movie that's two hours long? But those five little minutes can corrupt. Think about it this way: What if I were to offer you a plateful of mouthwatering brownies, but I put a little bit of dog poop in them? Would you want to eat them? Of course not! No matter how small an amount of dog poop is in the brownies, it still corrupted the whole batch. The same principle is true with impurity. No matter how insignificant it may seem, it still corrupts our whole being.[4]

> The only way we'll be able to produce pure fruit is to fill our hearts with God's Word.

There's no doubt that God has set high standards of purity—Jesus said that anyone who looks at someone with lust has already committed adultery in his or her heart (see Matt. 5:28)! I don't know about you, but I find that it's easy to get caught up in lustful thoughts without even realizing what's happening. I've discovered that it's impossible to live in purity on my own. But that doesn't mean I give up.

As flawed human beings, we're going to fail. David confirms this fact when he asks in Psalm 119:9, "How can a young man keep his way pure?" Immediately he answers his own question: "by living according to your word." He goes on in verse 11 to give us the secret to success in our battle against sin and impurity: "I have hidden your word in my heart, that I might not sin against you."

It doesn't take a rocket scientist to realize that the only way we'll be able to produce pure fruit is to fill our hearts with God's Word. Galatians 5:22-24 says:

The Holy Spirit produces this kind of fruit in our lives: love, joy, peace, patience, kindness, goodness, faithfulness, gentleness, and self-control. There is no law against these things! Those who belong to Christ Jesus have nailed the passions and desires of their sinful nature to his cross and crucified them there.

Wow! Talk about a great promise! If you're feeling as if you've failed miserably at guarding your heart, remember that if you've accepted Jesus Christ as your Savior, your sinful nature was nailed to the cross of Calvary and you no longer have to live in bondage. Jesus doesn't want you to just "get by" in life—He wants you to be victorious in the battle against your flesh.

One of the ways to do that is to ask Him to be the guardian of your heart. Allowing God to be the guardian of your heart is not just another important part of your spiritual growth; it is crucial. In fact, if you haven't already, I urge you to not let another day pass until you do!

Living a lifestyle of purity is far from easy. But let's not forget God's promise that it's worth it. In John 16:33, Jesus warned His disciples, "In this world you will have trouble. But take heart! I have overcome the world." He also promised:

> Come to me, all you who are weary and burdened, and I will give you rest. Take my yoke upon you and learn from me, for I am gentle and humble in heart, and you will find rest for your souls. For my yoke is easy and my burden is light (Matt. 11:28-30).

The common understanding of the word "yoke" is a bar that binds two oxen together to pull a load, but it also refers to a rabbi's teachings. In Bible times, rabbis (Jewish religious teachers) were identified by their rules, and if people wanted to be considered followers of a certain rabbi, they had to memorize and live by his "yoke." The regulations were often too heavy for people to bear, but Jesus said that His rules are easy—because He gives us the strength to follow them.

I'm not gonna lie to you: It's not painless to live a life of purity. It's difficult and often very lonely, but we don't have to do it on our own. We do it in the strength and power of our Savior, who has overcome the world!

Teach me your ways, O LORD, that I may live according to your truth! Grant me purity of heart, so that I may honor you (Ps. 86:11).

Notes

1. "Promiscuity," Wikipedia.org. http://en.wikipedia.org/wiki/Promiscuity (accessed February 2007).
2. Dictionary.com, s.v. "purity." *Dictionary.com Unabridged (v 1.0.1)*, based on the Random House Unabridged Dictionary (New York: Random House, Inc., 2006). http://dictionary.reference.com/browse/purity (accessed November 2006).
3. Frank Peretti, *The Oath* (Nashville, TN: Word Books, 1995).
4. Illustration from David Kirkwood in his short story, "Chocolate Brownies and Sin." http://imchurchmouse.lifewithchrist.org/permalink/25487 (accessed February 2007).

Chapter 4

Understanding Our Feelings and Emotions

Have you ever been in love? You know, the jolt of electricity when you hold hands with that special someone, the chills down your spine when he smiles at you, your heart skipping a beat when she enters the room? Sound familiar? Most everyone experiences these feelings at some point in their lives, and while they are fun and exhilarating, we're in for major problems if we base our relationships on them.

There's nothing wrong with experiencing the :-D and >:-(of a relationship. After all, we are tactile and emotional beings, and there *are* feelings associated with love. But the reality is, feelings are changeable and inconsistent, and if we build relationships based on them, our relationships will fall to pieces. Now please understand what I'm saying: The problem is not that we feel good when we're in a relationship. The problem is that we can become entangled in emotions when we follow our hearts instead of our heads.

In Matthew 7:26-27, Jesus told the story of a foolish person who built a house on the sand rather than a solid foundation. "The rain came down, the streams rose, and the winds blew and beat against that house, and it fell with a great crash" (v. 27). While Jesus was talking about the foolishness of not following His words, the crashing house is also a startlingly accurate picture of what happens to human relationships that are built on feelings. I don't know about you, but I don't want to be foolish and build a relationship that will come crashing down around me.

> We can become entangled in emotions when we follow our hearts instead of our heads.

So is there a way to make sure we are building our relationships on solid ground and guarding our hearts in the process? I believe there is. It hasn't been easy, but I've learned a few lessons about choices that make a difference. I think they might help you, too.

Choosing Faith over Feelings

I've been in full-time music ministry from a very early age—my family has literally traveled the world singing in churches and at conferences, conventions and crusades. As a result, my high school experience was rather unique. While most kids were studying for an algebra exam or sitting through yet another pop quiz in history class, I was traveling the country sharing the gospel through music. Of course, schoolwork was a part of my daily schedule, but I wasn't in a classroom five days a week.

Despite being in a close, loving family who loved the Lord and had a desire to share the gospel, life wasn't perfect. In March 2000, I spiraled down into a dark pit of depression.

Four months earlier, my world was turned upside down when my father and sister were hit head-on by a semi-truck. It was a 90-mile-an-hour impact, and both the car and truck were totaled. My mother and I were told that neither my father nor my sister, Heather, would survive.

I'll never forget entering that hospital. We could hear Heather's blood-curdling screams even before we got through the emergency room doors. I was 15 at the time, but in many ways became an adult overnight because of the litany of life-or-death decisions my mom and I suddenly had to make. We were told that my dad's hips were crushed and that there was a 50-50 chance he would be paralyzed from the waist down. My sister's face had been literally ripped off, her left eye exposed, her tongue nearly completely severed. Her prognosis was grim. Every organ in her body was either badly bruised or lacerated and we were told she had only a very slim chance of survival. "If she makes it," her doctors told us, "she'll never be normal again."

A week after the accident, my sister was released from the hospital and ordered to be on bed rest at home. We thought it was way too soon for her to go home, but there was an epidemic of staph infection at the hospital and the risk of staying outweighed the benefits. Although we were unprepared and ill equipped, my mom and I became Heather's caregivers.

My mom and I spent the next four months traveling between the hospital and home as we juggled caring for both my dad and sister. We spent Christmas, the New Year and several birthdays at the hospital.

In the months that followed, God did more miracles than I can even begin to describe, and by April, my dad thought he was well enough to start traveling and giving concerts again. I didn't want to, but I could tell he was eager for things to "get back to normal." He was still in a wheelchair and couldn't do anything for himself, so Mom and I became both caregivers and roadies.

I thought I was coping with everything very well, given the circumstances, but I finally snapped. I started showing signs of anorexia and lost 20 pounds practically overnight. (On my five-foot-six, 120-pound frame, that was a lot.) I just couldn't handle the stress anymore.

At one of our first concerts back, I lost it. "There's no way I can go on stage and talk about how good God is!" I told my mom. "I don't feel it!"

That's when Mom told me something I've never forgotten. "Brienne," she said, "are you going to allow your feelings to dictate how you live, or are you going to choose to live by what you know to be true?"

> I have the choice to live according to what is true or according to how I feel.

Whether she realized it or not, that was exactly what I needed to hear. When I decided to act on what I knew to be true rather than on what I felt, I began to rise above my circumstances and conquer my feelings. Oh, I still had problems. It was more than a year before I worked out the eating disorder for good. It was an uphill battle, but every time I started to lose it again, I remembered what Mom had told me.

Those difficult times helped me learn a valuable lesson: I have the choice to live according to what is true or according to how I feel. If I want to be obedient to God, I choose what is true. This lesson applies to many areas of my life, particularly my relationships.

I'm not telling this story to toot my own horn—I know you may have been through things far worse than I—but to give an example of what it looks like to live by faith rather than feelings. You may not have faced an accident such as the one my family did, but pain is a common denominator and something that every single one of us deals with at one time or another. Regardless of the circumstances that trigger our feelings, the choice of our response is up to us.

The Difference Between Feelings and Emotions

It is difficult to choose to follow what we believe rather than what we feel when we give our feelings free rein and become emotionally involved. Let me explain what I mean.

Emotions and feelings are not the same. Bestselling author Donna Partow says, "Emotion is any of the ways in which one reacts to something without careful thinking."[1]

Think about the last time you felt angry and said something without thinking that you later regretted. Your "emotional" reaction led to pain and remorse because you didn't take time to think about your feelings before you acted— "emoted"—on them. You see, a feeling is a *spontaneous and involuntary* response to a person or event, while an emotion is a *conscious* response to that strong feeling. In essence, feelings affect thoughts, which affect emotions, which in turn affect actions. We don't have control over the involuntary feeling, but we are responsible for our emotional choices. This is what the Bible means when it says that whatever is in the heart determines what we say (see Luke 6:45).

> Feelings affect thoughts,
> which affect emotions, which
> in turn affect actions.

Just as our feelings are involuntary, our bodies react involuntarily when we experience a strong feeling. Think about the last time you got embarrassed—you may have started to stammer, sweat or blush, all of which are involuntary reactions. When you're afraid, your heartbeat may speed up or your muscles may tense, as if getting ready for a fight. When you're happy, you may experience a sensation of lightness, as if you're "walking on air." Sadness is usually associated with feelings of tightness in the throat and eyes or extreme fatigue, and desire can be accompanied by a dry throat and heavy breathing.

These are outward manifestations of internal feelings, and while we are not able to control them, we *can* control the emotions that result. For example, it's perfectly normal to feel afraid of something, but when we allow that fear to give way to the emotion of aggression, we make a choice that may have negative consequences. The same goes for a feeling of desire that becomes the emotion of lust, or a feeling of sadness that becomes the emotion of bitterness.

Conscious emotions and actions start with involuntary feelings. When we allow our spontaneous feelings to dictate our emotions, we can hurt ourselves and other people. It's very important to learn how to think through our feelings so that we can wisely control our emotions. In other words, we need to learn to think before we act.

The Dangerous Side of Emotions

I'll be the first to admit that I'm a hopeless romantic—all my friends will attest to this fact. I turn to mush when I watch a good chick flick. I'm like many other girls who dream about having a boyfriend . . . getting married someday . . . having a family . . . and all that other gooshy stuff. And while I want the excitement of romance, I've realized there is a lot more to a relationship than two-dozen red roses and last-minute trips to Paris.

Finding Mr. or Mrs. Right takes a lot of prayer and patience, but when we get caught up in the emotion of a romance, it is very difficult to think carefully about our actions. We may *feel* we have a great relationship when what we really have are exciting feelings. I don't know about you, girls, but I don't want to be swept off my feet, feeling as if I've found the man of my dreams, and end up with a scummy guy who had a few good pick-up lines. Or guys, do you really want to pursue a pretty face and hot body only to find that she's meaner than a hungry tiger who hasn't gotten its beauty rest?

Feelings can't be trusted. And building a relationship on feelings—no matter how exciting they are—is a recipe for disaster. The Bible tells us a story in 2 Samuel 13 about the destruction that can result. In the short version, Prince Amnon fell in love with his half sister, Tamar. Rather than carefully considering his feelings, thinking through his emotions and actions, he allowed them to run wild to the point that he became physically ill.

> Building a relationship on feelings—no matter how exciting they are— is a recipe for disaster.

His friend Jonadab concocted a plan for Amnon to see Tamar privately—something that was nearly impossible to do in the palace. When they were alone, he asked her to have sex with him. When Tamar refused, Amnon raped her. The Bible says that after he violated her, his love turned to hatred and he hated her more than he ever loved her. The end of the story is brutal:

"Get out of here!" Amnon snarled at her.

"No, no!" Tamar cried. "Sending me away now is worse than what you've already done to me."

But Amnon wouldn't listen to her. He shouted for his servant and demanded that she be thrown out and the door locked behind her (vv. 15-17).

We all know that not every romance based on feelings ends this way, but this is a very real portrayal of what can happen when we allow our feelings to burn out of control and grow into uncontrollable emotions: Our actions can destroy lives.

God wants us to enjoy relationships with the opposite sex, but He wants us to do so in a way that protects our hearts. Relationships often start out completely pure and harmless, but as people become more and more emotionally connected, they can form unhealthy attachments. Shannon Ethridge and Stephen Arterburn explain the process of emotional connection in their book *Every Young Woman's Battle*:

- First we get the other person's *attention*
- Then we experience feelings of *attraction*
- Then we develop emotions of *affection* . . .
- Which can turn into an *attachment* . . .
- Which, left unchecked, can lead to *affairs* and even *addictions*[2]

It's a lot easier to protect our hearts and avoid unhealthy attachments when we recognize the different levels of emotional involvement and how they affect our hearts and actions. Unfortunately, my friends Jon and Allie had no idea how quickly feelings of mutual attraction could lead to irreversible involvement. Rather than controlling their emotional reactions to their feelings, they poured fuel on an already smoldering fire.

Choices that Lead to Emotional Attachment

Jon and Allie met on a mission trip and became fast friends. Over the course of the summer, they developed deeper feelings for each other and by the time the trip ended, they had become "an item."

Jon and Allie lived two and a half hours away from each other and they found it difficult to maintain the relationship once they went home. But they found ways to make it work, usually by spending hours and hours on the phone (mostly after midnight) and occasionally making the long drive to be together.

Over time, Jon realized that he and Allie were pushing the line. Both of them knew it was affecting their spiritual lives, but they felt trapped by their strong emotions.

They hadn't "gone all the way" yet, but they'd had plenty of chances to do so. One evening when Jon went to visit Allie, he ended up spending the night alone with her in her dorm room.

"We didn't do anything," he later told me, "but we came awfully close."

Jon and I are good friends, and he confessed the difficulties he was having in his relationship with Allie. I was frustrated for him because he didn't seem to realize that he was playing with fire. There wasn't much I could do except pray for them, especially after Jon told me they had become physically intimate.

> Whether we choose to control our emotions or allow them to run wild is up to us.

Jon and Allie eventually broke up. Jon was okay with it, but Allie was devastated. Jon was her first boyfriend, the first guy she had kissed, the guy she had given her virginity to. She was full of regret.

But their story didn't end there. I'll never forget the day Jon called me and said, "Uh . . . Brienne. I don't know how to tell you this, but . . . Allie and I got married last month. I thought it was the right thing to do because, well . . . Allie's pregnant."

Since then, I've talked to Jon and Allie on several occasions. They're working to deal with the consequences of the emotional connection they allowed to develop. Allie's trying to be a good wife and mother, but she's often said, "I wish someone would have told me to guard my heart before it was too late." She didn't realize that she was living by her feelings and allowing her emotions to control her actions. "It just felt so good," she told me. "I couldn't help myself."

Living by our feelings will get us into trouble, but we don't have to end up like Jon and Allie. Remember the lesson I learned about acting on what I *knew* to be true rather than on what I felt? We each must make that choice. Whether we choose to control our emotions or allow them to run wild is up to us.

Notes

1. Donna Partow, *Becoming the Woman I Want to Be* (Bloomington, MN: Bethany House Publishers, 2004), p. 11.
2. Shannon Ethridge and Steve Arterburn, *Every Young Woman's Battle* (Colorado Springs, CO: Waterbrook Press, 2004), n.p.

Avoiding the Emotional Roller Coaster

Does your mom or grandma ever bake cookies? I'm talking about moist, gooey, just-out-of-the-oven chocolate chip cookies—the kind you just can't wait to pick up and eat. You know how the smell wafts through the house, inviting you to come and sample one? The only problem is that they're so irresistible, we get burned in our hurry to taste them!

It's the same with relationships. Too many of us give in to the temptation to sample the warm, sweet benefits without stopping to consider the painful, burning consequences. We think, *It's just a little taste . . . it won't hurt anything.* But those "little tastes" stir up an appetite that can lead to pain and heartbreak.

During and after my relationship with Eric, I was an emotional basket case, and I found out later that he was just as bent out of shape, if not more. I had laid down some guidelines for myself, but he dove in head first, not even considering the consequences. Eric allowed himself to become so wrapped up in our relationship that he could no longer control his emotions—they ended up controlling him. At times he even became physically ill and was so distracted that he nearly failed tests.

Eric and I learned the hard way that when we give free rein to our emotions, we can cause ourselves a lot of pain. We didn't realize how important it is to be aware of where our emotions are leading us. We had no idea that when we indulge in emotional promiscuity or physical involvement, we're putting ourselves on an emotional roller coaster, a roller coaster that can be very difficult—if not impossible—to get off.

> When we indulge in emotional promiscuity, we're putting ourselves on an emotional roller coaster.

My friend Tom also learned this the hard way. Tom got saved in his early 20s, but because he had been a bit of a wild child, he wisely chose to stay single for the first five years after his conversion. Then, during his first year in college, he met The One. She was beautiful, fun and had a heart for ministry—everything a young pastor-in-the-making could hope for! Wanting to be cautious, Tom didn't pop the question right away. Instead, he watched Serena closely. He paid attention to her likes, her dislikes, her friends, her enemies. He prayed until he felt confident that she was someone with whom he could spend the rest of his life.

Tom didn't take their relationship casually. When he asked Serena if she would be his girlfriend, he told her that he wanted to date her with the intention of getting married. Serena was only too happy, and they began an idyllic summer romance. There was only one problem: Tom was several years older than Serena. It was only after they started dating that he realized just how immature she was. As they pursued their relationship, she started allowing her insecure emotions to get the best of her and admitted, "I just don't think I'm cut out to be a pastor's wife."

I met Tom when Serena was "taking a break." Her decision was devastating for him. As he expressed his frustrations to me, I tried to find where he had gone wrong. He'd been patient, he'd sought God's timing, he'd gotten to know her as a friend before adding romance.

It seemed as if Tom had done everything right—except one thing: He had given his heart away prematurely. As a result, he felt deeply wounded when things didn't go as planned because he had invested so much in the relationship on an emotional level.

Tom is still planning on being a pastor, but he's much more cautious about relationships than he used to be. "I don't know if I'll ever get married," he told me, "but I'm definitely going to be more careful with my emotions if and when I get involved with someone else."

Tom has allowed Jesus to fill the hole in his heart and is turning to his heavenly Father for comfort. Unfortunately, instead of turning to Jesus, many people try to fill the void with things that don't last or people who can't satisfy.

Although the relationship that initially broke her heart wasn't romantic, that's exactly what happened to my friend Justine.

The Miserable Couple
Who Couldn't Stand to Be Apart

Justine was abused as a little girl and abandoned by her father at a very young age. This left her with feelings of anger, distrust and a deep-seated emptiness—an emptiness she sought to fill in numerous ways. Understandably, Justine had a profound need to be loved. Relationships with guys helped for a while, but they didn't satisfy the deep longing within her—she didn't realize that God was the only One who could fill the void in her life and satisfy her need to "belong."

When she was 15, Justine started dating a guy named Matthew, who was 18 months older than she was. It was obvious to her youth pastor and friends that they weren't right for each other. They made each other exceptionally unhappy, but they couldn't keep their hands off each other. Besides the physical aspect of their relationship, there was absolutely nothing holding them together. They came to be known as "the miserable couple who can't stand to be apart." They were both so starved for love and affection that they just couldn't seem to break up.

Of course, their physical relationship made Justine and Matthew feel good about being together—that's part of what sex does—but they were so desperately needy for good feelings that they didn't filter those feelings through their minds. They didn't take their thoughts captive and control their actions, which is what God calls us to do (see 2 Cor. 10:5). They were wrapped up in emotion and blind to the dangers ahead . . .

Before long, Justine and Matthew began to isolate themselves from their friends because "no one understands us anymore." In reality, I think they felt convicted about the lack of purity in their relationship and didn't want to be held accountable for their actions. They had become addicted to their physical wants and desires, completely uncaring of anything and anyone else.

Matthew and Justine left their church and are now living together, completely entrenched in their sin. They "fell in love" with feeling good and chose to satisfy their need for genuine love with sex instead of God. They never learned the importance of allowing God to meet their needs and now live with terrible risks: depression, isolation, the risk of a broken heart, premarital pregnancy and STDs.

The Dangers of Following Your Heart

Before beginning a relationship, we need to consider if we're truly ready for the responsibility. Playing with love is no laughing matter, no matter how fun it might seem. Our emotions are more powerful than we realize and the old adage is still true today: If you play with fire, you're going to get burned. We must prepare our hearts and learn to bring our emotions under control. We must learn to satisfy the desires of our heart with Jesus, or we'll hurt ourselves or someone we care about.

> Playing with love is no laughing matter, no matter how fun it might seem.

We can't afford to forget the dire warning of Jeremiah 17:9: "The heart is deceitfully wicked." We can't rely on our hearts to lead us in the right direction because we'll get lost—every time. If you've ever seen the blockbuster movie *Pearl Harbor,* you know what I'm talking about. The film tells the story of two Army pilots who had been boyhood friends but who fall in love with the same woman. Evelyn is in love with Rafe, but when he is shot down over France and presumed dead, she turns to his best friend, Danny, for comfort. She ends up falling in love with him. Several months later, Rafe returns from behind enemy lines, longing to be with Evelyn—but on the very day he comes back, Evelyn discovers she is pregnant with Danny's baby.

Shortly after the Japanese attack on Pearl Harbor, both men are called on a secret mission to bomb Japan. Just before they leave, Evelyn tells Rafe that she is pregnant and plans to stay with the father of her child. "I'm going to give Danny my whole heart," she says, "but I don't think I'll ever be able to look at a sunset without thinking of you. I'll love you my whole life."

What a heart-wrenching illustration of the consequences of giving your heart away! *Pearl Harbor* may be just a movie, but the warning it presents is very real. Evelyn gave her heart to one man and her body to another, and discovered that she couldn't take either one back. The consequences of that decision haunted her for the rest of her life.

The decisions we make today will affect the rest of our lives, and because the heart is deceitfully wicked, we'll get hopelessly lost if we follow it. We will carry the scars of emotional wounds long after a relationship ends. Are you following God or are you following your heart?

Stopping to Consider

It's easy to give our hearts away without even thinking about it. When I was in eighth grade, my friend Haley started going out with a guy at our church. One Friday I spent the night at her house and we started talking about her boyfriend. I asked her what she liked about him and if she could see herself marrying him.

"No way!" she responded. "I could never marry Mark. We're just going out for the fun of it."

Her answer shocked me. I didn't understand why she would want to attach herself to someone knowing she'd only have to tear herself away. Haley may have thought their relationship was no big deal, but I saw how much time she and Mark spent together. Whether she realized it or not, her heart was involved, and I knew she was in for a big heartache when things ended.

God created us as sexual and emotional beings. He understands our feelings and desires, but He also wants to spare us from unnecessary hurt and pain. When we allow our hearts to run the show and our emotions to rage out of control, we shouldn't be surprised to find ourselves on the emotional roller coaster. We're not designed to give away our hearts promiscuously.

A lot of us jump on the roller coaster without even realizing it by engaging in fairly common activities like holding hands, cuddling on the couch or kissing. While they might seem harmless, these activities arouse feelings of connection and create an emotional bond that can be much more powerful and intimate than most people realize. If and when that bond is broken, it leaves a gaping hole that is not easily filled. God wants to hold our hearts and emotions steady, but the typical dating scene turns our emotions into one big roller-coaster ride: One minute we're soaring on top of the world, and the next it seems as if life isn't worth living.

> You hold something very special: the key to your heart.

Many of us can relate to jumping headfirst into a relationship without stopping to consider the consequences. It's just like that cookie: Sometimes we give in to the impulse to sample the sweetness and warmth we think we're missing—and burn our tongues in the process. And while a burnt tongue may not be life threatening, it sure is a painful reminder of our hastiness. The same holds true of relationships: We may not die of a broken heart, but we may have to endure a long and painful healing process.

You hold something very special: the key to your heart. God longs to help you protect it—your heart is precious to Him, and He doesn't want you to give it away to just anyone. But *you* hold the key. Will you unlock your heart and ride the first roller coaster that comes your way? Or will you give your key to God to protect until He brings Mr. or Mrs. Right into your life? The decision is up to you!

Protecting the Whole You

To win the Super Bowl, you have to know the playbook. To win on *Who Wants to Be a Millionaire*, you have to use your lifelines. To be a chess champion, you have to follow a strategy. To live pure lives, we need to know the Playbook, use our Lifeline and follow a strategy.

The good news is that God has given us a playbook in the form of the Bible. When it comes to purity, Proverbs 4:23 summarizes the message of the Playbook: "Guard your heart above all else, for it determines the course of your life." So how can we, as Christian young people, live up to the challenge? I don't claim to have all the answers, nor do I consider myself to have "arrived" in the area of guarding my heart. But I do know that God has a plan for your life, and how you use your Lifeline and follow through on your strategy makes all the difference.

God has given us a Lifeline through the still, small voice of the Holy Spirit. In the Gospel of John, Jesus said that the Holy Spirit will "convict the world of guilt in regard to sin and righteousness" (John 16:8, *NIV*). Not sure if your decision squares up with the Playbook? Use your Lifeline! (Pray!) God does not abandon us to find our way in the dark, but it's up to us to follow through on a strategy.

Paul wrote in his letter to the Philippians:

Don't worry about anything; instead, pray about everything. Tell God what you need, and thank him for all he has done (4:6).

The passage goes on to say that if we follow that strategy, we will experience God's perfect peace, peace that exceeds our wildest imagination (see v. 7). I don't know about you, but I've found life to be pretty confusing at times—the peace God gives is a welcome calm in the storm.

In order to play by the rules God has put in place and experience the peace and wellbeing that only He can give, we need to learn His Playbook, reach out for the Lifeline and follow His strategy for success. Let's dig a little deeper . . .

We Are Physical, Spiritual and Emotional Beings

God created us as three-part beings—body, soul, heart—and when we're out of balance in any of these areas, our whole state of wellbeing is threatened. We all know the importance of guarding our bodies, being physically fit, eating right and taking steps to protect ourselves from physical harm. But just how much attention do we give to feeding, exercising and guarding our hearts and spirits?

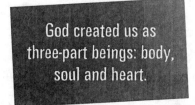

God created us as three-part beings: body, soul and heart.

What many of us don't realize is that our feelings produce emotional (heart), spiritual (spirit) and sexual (body) responses—so we need to thoughtfully rein in those feelings so that they lead to wholeness.[1] That's our strategy for living pure lives, and it fits perfectly with what Paul wrote in God's Playbook: "Stay away from every kind of evil" (1 Thess. 5:22). Paul knew that if left unchecked, our feelings can result in evil that affects us in every way—emotionally, spiritually and physically (that is, sexually). If we're not careful, this trio of responses can lead us into a confusing and deadly "Bermuda Triangle of Evil" in which we can become hopelessly lost.

I've come to appreciate the desire for wholeness that is reflected in Paul's prayer: "May the God of peace make you holy in every way, and may your whole spirit and soul and body be kept blameless until that day when our Lord Jesus Christ comes again" (1 Thess. 5:23). That's what God wants for us! If you're like me, however, it's really hard to maintain that balance in all three areas.

Have you ever experienced a spiritual "high" following church camp or a really awesome retreat? For a few weeks (or months, if you're lucky) you may feel holy, pure and on fire for God. Then real life sneaks back in and you begin to neglect the spiritual area of life.

Maybe you're really devoted to working out. Do you work hard to keep in tip-top physical shape but skip your morning devotions in order to have a few extra minutes at the gym?

Maybe you struggle with self-esteem and constantly try to find ways to be smarter or better looking. Maybe you struggle with self-condemnation and are continually beating yourself up for things over which you have no control. Or maybe you have a problem with self-mutilation and use cutting or starvation to drown out your feelings and emotions.

See how they are all related? We are spiritual, physical and emotional beings, and when one of these aspects is out of whack, all of them are affected. In order to be all that God wants us to be, we need to guard ourselves in all of these areas. Let's consider ways we can do that.

Guarding Our Souls

The spiritual side of this tricky triangle is something most of us seldom think about. When we accept Jesus into our lives, we say we are "asking Him into my heart," which directly links our hearts (emotions) with our spirituality. This means that when we fail to guard our hearts, we put our relationship with God at risk—we set ourselves up for a fall with serious consequences.

I recently learned that the original Hebrew word for "heart" actually refers to more than just the center of our feelings. In fact, it can be translated as "the inner person," which includes the mind, will and emotions. I think the reason Solomon was so adamant about telling us to guard our hearts was because he knew that the heart is both the door to our emotions *and* the window to our souls. As such, the heart directly affects our actions. When our inner being or heart is attacked, it affects our emotional, mental and spiritual health. In fact, my Tai Chi instructor suggests that it is the spirit that controls the mind, and the mind that controls our bodies, which is why it is so important to keep our spirits in tune with God.[2]

> When we fail to guard our hearts, we put our relationship with God at risk.

Before we become Christians, we are slaves to sin (see Rom. 6:16-22), which means our spirits are eternally separated from God. When we make the decision to surrender ourselves to Jesus, we are set free from sin—we are no longer slaves to impurity, but become "slaves" to righteousness. We establish the connection with God that He created us to have. However, whenever we sin, whether it's sexual promiscuity, pornography, drugs, alcohol, swearing, deceit—you name it—a wall is built between us and God, and that wall is not nearly as easy to tear down as it is to put up. Romans 8:7 actually says that "the sinful mind is hostile to God!" When we indulge in any kind of sexual, spiritual or emotional promiscuity, it severs our connection with God and makes it impossible to know or fulfill God's will for our lives.

It's no wonder that the apostle Paul, in Ephesians 4:17-19, says to stop living as the ungodly do: "Their minds are full of darkness; they wander far from the life God gives because they have closed their minds and hardened their hearts against him . . . They live for lustful pleasure and eagerly practice every kind of impurity." Paul may have been speaking to the ancient Ephesians, but he gives a shockingly accurate description of *our* world, and tells us what the Play is: *Stop living as the ungodly do.*

If we want to live in purity, we can't afford to fill our minds and hearts with darkness. We can't afford to wander from the life God gives us. Our strategy must be to make a conscious effort to guard our hearts. When we don't, our hearts become harder and harder until we reach a point of no return and can no longer discern purity from impurity.

Guarding Our Bodies

We're all aware of the physical risks (such as STDs and pregnancy) associated with premarital sex, but many of us don't realize the emotional implications of premature sexual involvement. Premarital sexual activity is inextricably connected to our emotions. In fact, it can lead to life-long struggles with anxiety, depression, paranoia, suicidal tendencies, anger management problems, anorexia and bulimia, social isolation, and a host of other emotional disorders. While physical and emotional reasons are valid and important, I think the most compelling argument for guarding ourselves sexually is found in Ephesians 5:3: "Let there be no sexual immorality, impurity, or greed among you. Such sins have no place among God's people." God's Playbook couldn't be clearer. He commands complete sexual purity among His children—no exceptions.

If we're going to live sexually pure lives, it's crucial that we have a strategy to prevent us from acting inappropriately on the basis of our hormones or feelings. First Thessalonians 4:3-5,7 outlines it for us:

> God's will is for you to be holy, so stay away from all sexual sin. Then each of you will control his own body and live in holiness and honor—not in lustful passion like the pagans who do not know God and his ways.

Other translations of this verse say, "It is God's will that you should be sanctified" (NIV), which means to be set apart, purified or made holy for a spiritual purpose. If we are set apart for a specific purpose, then we do not belong to ourselves—we belong to God and our decisions and behaviors need to reflect this fact (see 1 Cor. 6:19).

The realization that we belong to God is essential before we can keep our hearts, minds and bodies in check. The only way to live in true purity is to surrender every single part of our lives to Christ. This means truly offering our bodies as a living sacrifice to God as an act of worship. It means steadfastly refusing to conform to the patterns of the world and choosing instead to be transformed by the renewing of our minds (see Rom. 12:1-2).

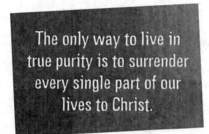

The only way to live in true purity is to surrender every single part of our lives to Christ.

Once we have made the crucial choices to belong to God and surrender ourselves to Him, we must be vigilant, conscious of the many ways in which we can stray from physical purity. We have to continually go back to God's Playbook for wisdom and guidance, and learn to think with our heads instead of our hearts.

Masturbation, for example, isn't often talked about in church, but recent studies suggest that as many as 80 percent of young people struggle with it (and some people claim the number is actually much higher). How do we deal with it? Society tells us that if it feels good, go for it—the mother of a friend of mine told her that whatever she does in the privacy of her own room is okay as long as she's not hurting herself. But the apostle Paul reminds us that we have been set apart for God's purpose and shows us the danger of such thinking:

> Run from sexual sin! No other sin so clearly affects the body as this one does. For sexual immorality is a sin against your own body. Don't you realize that your body is the temple of the Holy Spirit, who lives in you and was given to you by God? You do not belong to yourself, for God bought you with a high price. So you must honor God with your body (1 Cor. 6:18-20).

That's the bottom line. To honor God with our bodies means not only being completely pure in our physical relationships with the opposite sex but also *in every way*. I'll be the first to say that it's really hard to keep my body only for the Lord, especially when I think about how long it might be before I can righteously fulfill my sexual desires within the bonds of marriage. Yet the Bible says that there should not be even a hint of sexual immorality or any kind of impurity among God's people (see Eph. 5:3).

Guarding Our Thoughts

The mind is a wonderful thing. God created humans as the only living beings with a mind that can comprehend both logic and emotion and that can communicate in complex languages. We are the only living things with an imagination. Imagination can be a great thing, but it can also be deadly when it leads us to lustful temptations. One of my professors describes temptation as having three stages: desire (when we feel the initial draw to sin), conception (rationalizing sin) and development and bondage (little sins that pave the way for tomorrow's bondage).

Just think about how these stages play out in your thought life. It may start with normal sexual desire, which is spontaneous and involuntary. If left unchecked, however, desires can lead to harmful fantasies, which lead to emotions of sexual frustration and lust.

Just as our thought life affects our physical bodies, it also affects our emotions. Guarding what happens in our minds is essential to emotional purity. You may think of yourself as a sexually chaste person, but what do you think about? Watching television shows like *Laguna Beach* or *The Real World*, reading romance novels or visiting questionable websites might seem like minor indulgences, but have you ever stopped to consider what these activities are doing to your fantasy life? What is their impact on your thought life? Are they encouraging you to think things that are honorable and pure, or do they cause your mind to wander into sinful territory?

> Whoever controls your emotions controls you.

It's easy to overlook the impact of your thought life on your emotions. It's easy to forget that whoever controls your emotions controls you. It's easy to rationalize lustful thoughts or fantasies by thinking, "I'm not *doing* anything . . . I'm just having a little fun." But this is another instance in which God's Playbook must have the final word:

The LORD detests the thoughts of the wicked, but those of the pure are pleasing to him (Prov. 15:26, *NIV*).

Whenever we fail to guard ourselves physically, spiritually or emotionally, we can severely damage our communion with God and run the risk of losing our "compass." When this happens, every area of our life is thrown out of whack. God doesn't want to steal our fun. In fact, quite the opposite—He wants to protect us from ourselves and help us guard our hearts.

So what's the secret to guarding our hearts and achieving balance in all three areas of life? It's found in Matthew 22:37-38:

> Love the Lord your God with all your heart and with all your soul and with all your mind. This is the first and greatest commandment (*NIV*).

This simple command is the foundation on which we can build a winning strategy for purity.

Notes

1. Donna Partow, *Becoming the Woman I Want to Be* (Minneapolis, MN: Bethany House, 2004), p. 11.
2. Contrary to popular belief, Tai Chi is not associated with any pagan religion but is a sequence of meditative movements designed to foster balance between one's spirit, mind and body.

Setting Boundaries: Putting the Playbook into Practice

I'll never forget my sixteenth birthday. I started Drivers Ed. shortly after I turned 15, so I had been driving for nearly a year when my birthday finally rolled around— I was *more* than ready for the freedom that would accompany my license. We lived out in the country, and getting my license meant I would no longer have to miss out on social events or parties because I didn't have a ride. Having a license meant I could do what I wanted, when I wanted (or so I thought) . . . but as anyone who has been driving for any amount of time can tell you, I still had a lot to learn—not just about driving, but about the freedom that came with it.

Sixteen is not only the magic driving age, but it also seems to be the universal dating age. While I wanted a relationship with a guy, as my birthday approached I realized that I didn't want to end up in the cycle of meaningless relationships that is so often part of the junior high/high school scene. To avoid being caught in that cycle, I realized that I needed a strategy. I needed to create a plan to protect myself.

I decided to begin by drawing some boundary lines for myself. I started with the obvious lines, like not dating anyone who isn't a Christian, but I added some specifics that proved to be very important. My boundaries included not being alone with members of the opposite sex, not discussing intimate or personal details and feelings with members of the opposite sex, not dating someone I couldn't see myself marrying, and not becoming physically involved with someone I'm not engaged to.

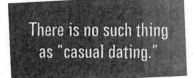

There is no such thing as "casual dating."

The boundary lines you draw for yourself may or may not look like the ones I drew. It is crucial, however, that you think about appropriate boundaries and start listing them. Those boundaries helped me think through my feelings and gave me the tools to help keep my emotions in check, and as a result, I avoided some very damaging emotional attachments that would have been extremely difficult to break.

I was fortunate to realize that dating is the process by which we determine our life partner, which is why I believe there is no such thing as "casual dating." Girls especially can't help but get emotionally involved. God designed men to protect and commit themselves to one woman, and made women to give themselves to one man, emotionally and physically.

Ladies, did you know that the hormone released during sex (oxytocin) is the same hormone released when a woman gives birth? It's a hormone that God designed in order for a mother to bond with her child and a wife to bond with her husband. That's part of the reason it's so hard for us to separate the physical from the emotional when we're in a relationship, and that is why it's so important to set boundaries and stick with them—regardless of our feelings and emotions.

Boundaries Are for Our Protection

Although my friends Shaun and Connie knew it was important to follow God's Playbook for life and relationships, they didn't realize they needed a strategy to put it into practice. They didn't realize how important it is to set boundaries as part of that strategy, and they paid a very high price for their ignorance.

Shaun was raised in a Christian home but got in with the wrong crowd in junior high and started experimenting with drugs and alcohol. From there, things got worse. As he entered his teens, he had numerous relationships with girls, none of which lasted very long. He accepted Christ when he was 17, and we became friends soon after his conversion. Since then, it has been a daily struggle to overcome his old nature and habits, a struggle he admits he often loses.

One summer Shaun began dating a girl he met at camp. They both knew they were getting too physically involved but didn't have the motivation or the knowledge to stop it. As time went on, their physical relationship got more and more heated—the temptation to become sexually intimate grew with each passing day. Shaun knew he couldn't keep his old nature in check on his own, so he grabbed a Lifeline. He asked for my help in setting boundaries for himself.

Knowing his past weaknesses, I suggested that he and Connie never be alone together at night. I strongly discouraged him from spending the night at her house, even if her parents were home. I also suggested that he limit the amount of time they spent on the phone. Keeping those boundaries was up to Shaun.

Not long after, Connie's dad went out of town. Ignoring my advice, Shaun decided to spend the night at her house. The temptation was too much for them—they took their relationship where they hadn't gone before. Shaun allowed his sinful nature to live freely within him and in a moment of weakness, he deliberately crossed the barriers he had put in place to protect both Connie and himself.

> God doesn't tell us not to have premarital sex to keep us from having fun, but to keep us from destroying ourselves from the inside out.

Even before the infamous night at Connie's house, Shaun knew something was wrong with their relationship, and he had doubts about whether or not he and Connie should continue to see each other. Even though he had started to put a plan in place to prevent things from getting out of hand, he allowed his feelings and emotions to rage out of control. He thought he was strong enough to stand up to temptation, but in the heat of the moment, he abandoned his strategy and paid a very high price.

God doesn't tell us not to have premarital sex to keep us from having fun, but to keep us from destroying ourselves from the inside out. When a man and a woman are married and join together in sexual relations, the Bible says they become one flesh (see Gen. 2:24). Connie and Shaun violated that order and joined their bodies together before God had joined their hearts in holy matrimony. Shortly after that, their relationship began to fall apart.

Shaun and Connie's relationship ended in devastation. Connie had given Shaun a treasure she can never take back, and Shaun had once again fallen prey to his old nature. He built a wall between himself and God by putting himself in a compromising situation that he wasn't strong enough to resist.

Giving God Control

God wants to write a beautiful love story for each of us, but in order for Him to do that, we have to be willing to give Him the pencil—and sometimes the eraser. I'll never forget the night God asked me to do just that. I was doing my devotions in my room when I felt the Holy Spirit gently tug on my heart.

"Brienne," He said. "You've been trying to control your life, rather than allowing Me to do My job. If you really love Me, you will trust Me to take care of your future."

This may not seem like a big deal to you, but you have to understand how much it rocked me. You see, I'm one of those focused, ambitious kids who had mapped out my future by age nine. I had chosen the schools where I would earn my undergraduate and master's degrees, my profession (and hobbies), my wedding colors and names for my children. If there was something that could be planned out, I had done it.

I had tried to figure everything out on my own, but instead of my little plan, God had another one. And as difficult as it was to turn my life plans over to Him, I'm so glad I did. God has reshaped, reformed and added to my original plan in ways I could never have imagined. When I look back at my plans, they pale in comparison to what God has done and is continuing to do.

Giving God the eraser and telling Him that He could erase anything I had already planned that wasn't a part of

His perfect plan was the scariest thing I'd ever done. But giving Him the pencil (or permanent marker!), and telling Him to write whatever He wanted was the most liberating thing I've ever done.

Boundaries I Missed

I share this part of my life story because it demonstrates that no matter how committed we are to following God's will for our lives, we're not going to do it perfectly. We're going to mess up; we're going to miss things that should have been obvious to us. Even though I surrendered to God's plan for my life, there were many times that I messed up and took the pencil and eraser back—but every time, He gently reminded me of that night and helped me to surrender my will to His once more.

Less than two weeks after that life-changing night in my relationship with God, my relationship with Eric got started. We were on our way back from camp, and I realized there was more to this guy than I'd previously thought. When we first met, he was the typical class clown, willing to do anything for a laugh. But as we started talking on the bus, I began to see a deeper side of him, one I hadn't seen before.

As the summer progressed, we started talking more frequently. Little by little, some of the boundaries I had so carefully laid out began to crumble. I started thinking of our relationship as being exclusive, and Eric became possessive and would get jealous if he saw me talking to any other guys in the youth group. We spent way too much time talking online, and I found myself "stretching the truth" with my parents about who I was IMing—I didn't want them to know it was Eric. We also developed code words so that we could talk to each other without other people knowing what we were saying. While each of these things may not seem like a big deal, I was breaking the barriers I had specifically put in place in order to protect my heart. I got so caught up in my feelings that I allowed those feelings to fuel my emotions and control my actions.

So where did I go wrong with Eric? Everything comes back to motives and heart attitude: Did I truly want God to protect my heart and emotions, or was I saying one thing and doing something entirely different? The bottom line is that even though I said I wanted God to protect my heart, my actions took me in the opposite direction.

I learned the hard way that knowing the Playbook and setting boundaries aren't enough. We have to be willing to *do* what the Playbook says and *stay* within those boundary lines.

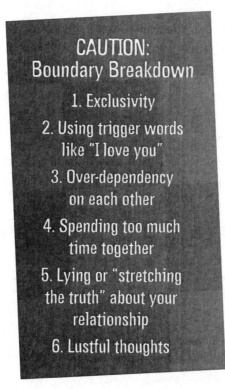

CAUTION:
Boundary Breakdown

1. Exclusivity
2. Using trigger words like "I love you"
3. Over-dependency on each other
4. Spending too much time together
5. Lying or "stretching the truth" about your relationship
6. Lustful thoughts

Setting Boundaries that Lead to Mr. or Mrs. Right

In her book *When God Writes Your Love Story*, Leslie Ludy describes her dream guy as "someone who treats me like a princess, someone who is sensitive, tender, gentle, brave, full of integrity, servant hearted, and honorable." She goes on to say how she thought she was looking for Prince

Charming until a friend told her to think about all the qualities she had mentioned.

"Leslie," her friend said. "Who can you think of that is a *perfect example* of all those character traits?"

"Um . . . Superman?" Leslie guessed.

"No" said her friend. "Jesus Christ. Those desires for that kind of a man have been in your heart from a young age. But you are not the one that came up with those longings. It was God who put them in your heart, because He wants you to look for a man with the character of Jesus Christ!"[1]

If we're supposed to be looking for someone with the character of Jesus, why do we allow ourselves to become emotionally wrapped up in relationships that are leading nowhere? Too many of us spend our time wondering when "Prince Charming" will sweep us off our feet or when the "Ultimate Dreamgirl" will walk through the door, when instead, we need to be living in the Word, meditating on God's promises and working on becoming the godly man or woman that our future spouse needs us to be. God's Playbook makes the way clear:

> Commit everything you do to the LORD. Trust
> him, and he will help you. He will make your inno-

cence radiate like the dawn, and the justice of your cause will shine like the noonday sun (Ps. 37:5-6).

When I gave my dating life completely over to God, I started to make a list of the things I wanted in a guy. It's changed a little over the years, but these characteristics have remained consistent:

I want a guy who . . .

1. Puts God first
2. Is passionate in his worship and prayer times
3. Is a sensitive and compassionate listener
4. Takes the initiative
5. Is a strong leader
6. Is not afraid of what people think
7. Is a gentleman
8. Is respectful of authority
9. Strives for excellence
10. Shares my desire for full-time ministry

You'll notice that my list doesn't include any physical characteristics. That's intentional. It's not that I don't want to marry an attractive man, but I've come to realize that sparkling teeth, wavy hair and bulging arms are of little importance when compared to someone's character. Paying attention to this list helps me to protect my heart by reminding me what God's best looks like.

You may think my standards are too high. (I've been told that on more than one occasion.) One friend told me flat out, "Brienne, there is no such thing as Prince Charming." But I'm not looking for Prince Charming—I'm looking for God's best! Part of knowing the Playbook is recognizing the boundaries that God has already put in place to protect us from Mr. or Mrs. Wrong.

Setting Boundaries in Friendships and Dating Relationships

How many times have you heard someone say, "We're just friends" and rolled your eyes thinking, *Sure you are.* It's really sad, but very few relationships with a person of the opposite sex remain platonic. Most of the time, one of the parties develops deeper feelings for the other person, which can lead to awkwardness and resentment if the feelings aren't reciprocated.

I wouldn't say it's impossible to be "just friends," but I only see it happen on rare occasions. Too often, a person's self esteem is shattered and his or her emotions torn apart because the closeness of the friendship leads to feelings of being "in love" that are rejected by the other person. Even if you're really good friends with someone, it's still important to make sure you set boundaries to ensure that your friendship remains completely pure and above board.

With my guy friends, I try to make sure that I'm not flirtatious or touchy-feely in a way that could send a mixed message. I'm also very careful with the subjects I talk about and cautious about sharing things that are overly personal.

On those occasions when an acquaintance or friendship does lead to a dating relationship, it's even more important to set appropriate boundaries. Too many couples find themselves in trouble because they don't think ahead and get caught up in the feelings and emotions. The only way to avoid trouble is to set standards ahead of time and to refuse to waver. In fact, don't just set your standards ahead of time—make sure your date knows your standards and shares your convictions.

Before you begin a relationship, decide what you are and are not willing to do. This should be done *on your own*, not with your boyfriend or girlfriend. While it is a good idea to discuss your standards with the person you're dating, discuss your boundaries and strategies and then leave it at that. If you talk about your boundaries over and over again, your mind is likely to wander and you may be more inclined to compromise.

> Set standards ahead
> of time and refuse
> to waver.

Finally, when you determine what a boundary is, write it down. It's a lot harder to waver if things are set in black and white. Here's a beginning strategy I would suggest using:

- I will only date a Christian (see 2 Cor. 6:14).
- I will concentrate on building a solid friendship before I advance into romance.
- I will not purposely flirt—it may be fun for me, but it isn't treating my "brother or sister" with love (see 1 Tim. 5:1-2).

- I will not be alone with a member of the opposite sex in either my home or theirs. I will avoid sitting in cars and closed rooms and will limit alone time to public places (see 1 Thess. 5:22).
- I will refrain from tickling, back rubs or other forms of physical touch.

You may be afraid to set things out this frankly because you may think that setting boundaries will stifle your relationship or scare off a great guy or girl. Nothing could be farther from the truth! When my friend Darla and her boyfriend Michael started dating, he told her that they were going to do it right and then laid out all the rules for their relationship: no physical involvement, accountability to their parents and friends, limited alone time, and so on. Let me tell you, no guy ever gained more points faster! In that one conversation, Michael gave Darla more security and comfort than any guy she had ever known. She knew he truly wanted to love and protect her because he had a strategy to make sure that their relationship didn't cross any boundaries.

The bottom line is that it's impossible to have any healthy, male-female relationship without putting boundaries in place. Rather than waiting until we're in the heat of the moment, we need to realize the multi-level benefit of boundaries and put them in place *before* we find ourselves in a compromising situation. Read on to discover more ways to go into a relationship with your eyes wide open and protect the heart your heavenly Father treasures . . .

Note
1. Eric and Leslie Ludy, *When God Writes Your Love Story* (Colorado Springs, CO: Multnomah Publishers, 2004), pp. 163-164.

Dos and Don'ts: The Tools for Guarding Your Heart

I'm not going to weigh in on one side or the other of the dating vs. courtship debate. The fact is, guy/girl relationships are a part of our culture. I've read most of the "dating" books, and I'm not nearly as concerned about what we label our relationships as I am about how we live out our faith and convictions in whatever type of relationships we find ourselves. I personally have chosen to steer clear of the casual dating scene that our society accepts as normal because of my conviction about living my faith out in relationships, and I'm troubled by the assumption that as long as we don't "go all the way" we're okay. If we want to live truly pure lives, it's imperative that we focus our attention on how we can guard our hearts and protect ourselves from the pain of all types of premature intimacy.

God is very clear and specific about how He wants us to live in relationship with Him and one another. The Bible, His Playbook, gives us plenty of guidelines and examples, but it's up to us to execute the plan God has outlined for us. Although we may not like them, Dos and Don'ts are necessary for preserving purity. They are the tools that help us do what the Playbook says.

> Dos and Don'ts are tools that help us maintain a relationship with God and live at the center of His will.

God doesn't give us Don'ts to prevent us from having fun—Don'ts are God's boundaries that enable us to live life to the fullest. Notice how the apostle Paul addresses this very issue in his letter to the Corinthians:

> I want you to be free from the concerns of this life . . . I am saying this for your benefit, not to place restrictions on you. I want you to do whatever will help you serve the Lord best, with as few distractions as possible (1 Cor. 7:35).

That's why we have Dos and Don'ts: They help us live pure lives of service to God. But we must be careful that we don't start thinking of the Christian life as being about what we do or don't do. *The Christian life is about having a relationship with God.* Dos and Don'ts are tools that help us maintain that relationship with God and live at the center of His will.

Let's take a look at some principles from God's Playbook and consider the Dos and Don'ts we need to put into practice to live in purity.

Important Dos

The number one Do for any relationship is to *put God first.* It may seem obvious, but I'm surprised by how many people forget this foundational element. If you want a successful relationship, God must be at the center of it.

How do we put God first? We spend time with Him on a daily basis. We pray—and I don't mean occasional shotgun prayers! I mean serious conversations with God about our desires and concerns and His desires and concerns (see chapter 12 for more details). We beg Him to keep us in the center of His will, which may mean getting on our faces before Him in intercessory prayer (see chapter 13). It may mean we go that extra mile to fast, showing God that we are really serious about our petitions and practicing self-denial before we're between a rock and a hard place. It may even mean sacrificing something we love because we are distracted from hearing God's voice and following His direction.

Once God is first, we need to *live in the light* of our relationship with Him. First John 1:7-8 tells us that if we are living in the light as God is in the light, we have fellowship with each other and the blood of Jesus will cleanse us from all impurity. But "if we claim we have no sin, we are only fooling ourselves and not living in the truth" (v. 8). How do we live in the light? *We live according to what is true.*

If we're not walking in the light (that is, if we're living a secret life), we're deceiving ourselves if we don't think we're giving in to temptation. God, on the other hand, is not deceived—He is brutally honest about the truth. Jesus said, "anyone who even looks at a woman with lust has already committed adultery with her in his heart" (Matt. 5:28). *THE MESSAGE* puts this verse this way:

> Don't think you've preserved your virtue simply by staying out of bed. Your heart can be corrupted by lust even quicker than your body. Those leering looks you think nobody notices—they also corrupt.

Whoa! Talk about a strong statement! There's no hiding from the truth in that one.

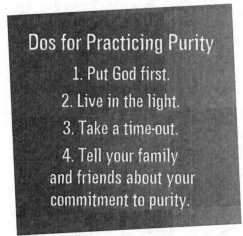

Dos for Practicing Purity
1. Put God first.
2. Live in the light.
3. Take a time-out.
4. Tell your family and friends about your commitment to purity.

Let's make it practical: If Jesus were to walk into your life right now, how do you think He would react to what you're doing, and how might He feel about what is happening in your heart and mind? Would you be embarrassed? Would your pastor be disappointed by the level of physical intimacy you enjoy with your boyfriend or girlfriend? If your future spouse was watching you on a late night movie date, or in the backseat of your car, or on the front step when you're "just saying goodnight," do you think he or she would feel treasured and loved?

If your thought life or behavior can't stand up to the light of God's presence, you need to consider that you're probably not living in true purity.

It is always best to avoid compromising situations, but should you find yourself in dangerous territory, don't be afraid to *take a time-out* when necessary. Even though we can't help our feelings, we *can* take the necessary steps to keep those feelings from fueling our emotions. The next time you find yourself in the middle of a heated situation, remember that it's okay to take a step back and reevaluate.

Absolutely, Positively, Always Avoid . . .

If we're going to guard our hearts, we have to be willing to give up some things, and one of those is the freedom to date a non-Christian. The single quickest way to get yourself in trouble is to be in a relationship with someone whose convictions are different from your own. If you are constantly being pressured to compromise, sooner or later you'll get tired and give in. However, if you are both working toward the same goal, the chances are a lot better that you will successfully guard your purity. So the first Don't is to avoid dating a non-Christian, or anyone whose convictions differ from your own.

Next: Absolutely, positively, always *avoid secluded places and intense alone time.* Some people argue that putting yourself in difficult situations builds character, but I've found many flaws with this philosophy. The greatest flaw is that putting yourself in difficult situations is opposed to the instructions in God's Playbook:

> Flee the evil desires of youth, and pursue righteous-
> ness, faith, love and peace, along with those who
> call on the Lord out of a pure heart (2 Tim. 2:22).

Notice the first word: *Flee!* It doesn't say try it out first, put yourself to the test or sit and think about it and then walk away when you get bored. It says to *flee,* which means to run away as fast and far as you can.

Too many of us think we are strong enough to resist the temptations of being alone together. I don't care who you are or who you are dating, if you make it a habit to be at your girlfriend's or boyfriend's house alone late at night, sexual and emotional promiscuity will happen, even if only in your mind (and the mind is the biggest sex organ in the body).

Are you fleeing the evil desires of youth or are you allowing your feelings and emotions to control you?

If it's the latter, I challenge you to step up to the plate as a man or woman of God and make a commitment to rise above your feelings and start living by the Word of God. As long as we allow our emotions to control us, we are defenseless against the fiery darts of the enemy. But when we make the decision to live by what we know to be true (remember, *live in the light*), we can take back ground the enemy has stolen.

> The lies of Satan are capable of destroying us, but we don't have to fall for them!

Satan has been lying to people since the Garden of Eden. That's why 1 Peter 5:8 tells us to "Stay alert! Watch out for your great enemy, the devil. He prowls around like a roaring lion, looking for someone to devour." The lies of Satan are capable of destroying us, but we don't have to fall for them! First John 4:4 tells us that we have already won the victory because "the Spirit who lives in you is greater than the spirit who lives in the world."

So what are Satan's lies? One of his favorites is that there's no harm in just looking. Don't ever believe it! *Don't convince yourself that "just looking" is okay.* Daytime soap operas and romance novels encourage women to fantasize sexually, while the Internet has crossed a new frontier in providing guys with images to fuel their fantasies into a blazing inferno. Why is "just looking" such a huge market? Because the hormones released during sexual arousal can become just as addicting as many illicit drugs. If left unchecked, seemingly harmless fantasies can lead to a lifetime of unhealthy relationships, emotional turmoil and sexual addiction.

Sometimes "just listening" can lead to problems as well, so I believe it is imperative to *avoid talking late at night.* This includes spending time alone together, talking on the phone and online chats. Late at night, we say things that we wouldn't usually say, and we're more susceptible to falling into the trap of emotional promiscuity. When we're tired, we lower our guard. We have a tendency to be a lot more vulnerable.

In addition to setting boundaries for *when* you talk, you should also set boundaries for *what* you talk about. Discussing personal topics such as relationships, sex, making out (or anything along those lines) with a member of the opposite sex can cause our minds to wander in places they don't need to go.

This next one may sound counterintuitive, but it's imperative to absolutely, positively, always *avoid one-on-one prayer time*. We know that putting God first in our relationships is good and that prayer is an important part of putting God first, so we might naturally assume that praying together must be a good thing in a relationship. Sounds nice on paper, but it's risky in practice.

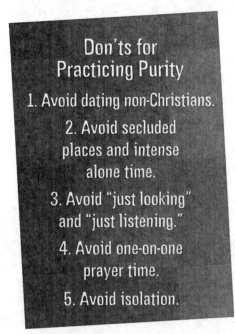

Don'ts for Practicing Purity

1. Avoid dating non-Christians.

2. Avoid secluded places and intense alone time.

3. Avoid "just looking" and "just listening."

4. Avoid one-on-one prayer time.

5. Avoid isolation.

Prayer is an incredibly intimate and vulnerable thing that can lead to emotional entanglements. It not only draws us closer to God, but it also draws us closer to the person with whom we are praying—and that can lead to premature intimacy. I'm not saying you shouldn't pray for someone, but praying *for* someone and praying *with* someone are two very different things. Reserve praying together for when a relationship reaches the point of moving toward marriage—otherwise you can find yourself in some sticky situations.

It's also important to *avoid isolation.* Anytime a relationship gets too exclusive or a couple starts isolating themselves from family or friends, they're headed for trouble. Satan would love to make you think that no one understands you or that you're the only one who struggles with the temptations you face, but the Bible is very clear about the importance of Christian fellowship and accountability. First Peter 5:9 explicitly tells us to stand firm in our faith, remembering that our brothers and sisters around the world are enduring the same things we are, and 1 Corinthians 10:12-13 confirms that we are not alone:

> If you think you are standing strong, be careful not to fall. The temptations in your life are no

different from what others experience. And God is faithful. He will not allow the temptation to be more than you can stand. When you are tempted, he will show you a way out so that you can endure.

Talk About It!

Christian fellowship and accountability are important tools in maintaining purity in our walk with God. Deuteronomy 6:6-8 tells us to talk about the things God is doing in our lives, and by following those instructions, we not only encourage other people, but we also advocate accountability. It is a huge encouragement to hear about the things that God is doing. Even more important, when we're focusing on the things of God and the standards by which He wants us to live, it's a lot harder for our minds to wander into dangerous territory.

I can't stress how important it is to *tell your family and friends about your commitment to purity*. It's a whole lot harder to become emotionally entangled if you have other people holding you accountable. It is much easier to guard your heart from the harm that comes from crossing the line when you know someone will hold you accountable to your strategy.

I consider myself very blessed to have the parents I have. I know that I can go to them with any question or problem, and if they don't have the answer, they will seek God until they find it. But I realize that not everyone has that option. For some reason or another you may not be able to confide in your parents. (Let me be clear: Discounting your relationship with your parents because "They don't understand me!" is not what I'm talking about here. If you make a serious effort to share your thoughts and feelings, you may be surprised at how wise they really are! Give them a chance.)

However, if you aren't able to be accountable to your parents for one reason or another, that doesn't mean you can't be accountable to someone. There are plenty of people you can go to for guidance and accountability, such as your pastor/pastor's wife or youth pastor/youth pastor's spouse. Not only is it their job to guide you in your faith, I guarantee they will be thrilled to help you maintain purity in your relationships.

If you don't feel comfortable or are unable to go to your pastor or youth pastor, ask God to send you a mentor or accountability partner. I did just that, and at a time in my life when I needed it most, God brought me a wonderful woman who has helped me in more ways than I can say.

She's a bit older than I am (she is married and has three kids), but she is younger than my mother. She is sort of an in-between person—older and wiser than my girlfriends, yet still close enough to my age to understand what I'm going through.

Although fellowship and accountability are very important, I need to mention two cautions. First, for obvious reasons, accountability partners must be of the same gender. Second, although our first instinct is to go to our friends to spill our guts and ask for advice, I recommend doing so only as a last resort. It's great to talk to our friends about our problems, but they're at the same place in life that we are—their advice is likely to be quite limited. Seeking wisdom from someone who has already walked in our shoes (rather than from someone who *is* walking in our shoes—tripping over the same rough spots that send us sprawling) is the best way to get great advice and be understood and respected.

The Recipe for Purity?

In spite of all the Dos and Don'ts for following God's instructions for purity, there is no recipe for the perfect relationship. We can read all the books (and believe me,

I have!), attend motivational conferences, listen to inspirational speakers, even read the Bible—but the only "formula" is living a pure life:

> Don't copy the behavior and customs of this world, but let God transform you into a new person by changing the way you think. Then you will learn to know God's will for you, which is good and pleasing and perfect (Rom. 12:2).

The only way we will ever have truly pure relationships in life is to take our relationship with God seriously. We seek His will for our life and relationships. We pray and ask Him to renew our minds daily. We repent of our failures and ask Him to restore whatever innocence has been lost or given away. And we are diligent to make full use of the tools He's given us for guarding our hearts.

Waiting for God's Best

Between cell phones, IMs, DSL, e-mail, Google, TiVo and credit cards, we don't have to wait for anything anymore. Everything we could ever want is available right at our fingertips. And even if we can't afford it, we can buy now and pay later!

As a society and as individuals, we have become so accustomed to instant gratification and living in the moment that we seem to have forgotten that waiting isn't necessarily a bad thing. But let's think about it for a minute. Aren't some things worth waiting for?

As a kid, I looked forward to Christmas like a bride for her wedding day. Mom knew just what to do to make Christmas special—we spent the whole month of December getting ready for the big day. We put up Christmas decorations, played Christmas music, read Christmas stories, made Christmas cookies and shopped for Christmas presents. And of course, every year I looked under the tree and shook every present that had my name on it. Sometimes I even tried to peek under the wrapping to see what might be inside! But I never went so far as to open a present early. When Christmas morning came and I was finally able to open my presents, I was always surprised and very thankful that I had waited. Waiting in anticipation for the right moment was part of what made the gifts and the celebration so special.

There is a "first time" for many different things, but there is never more than one first time. If I had opened a Christmas gift before Christmas morning and then wrapped it up and put it back under the tree, no one would have known but me. But I would have missed out on the thrill of eager expectation *and* on the first-time delight of Christmas Day. It would have been much less exciting (and perhaps even disappointing) to open presents I had already seen.

Do Not Stir Up

In the Bible, the book of Song of Solomon (sometimes called "Song of Songs") tells the beautiful story of a romance that developed between a shepherd girl and King Solomon. It tells of their struggle to remain pure and how they recognized the need to save themselves for marriage. The statement "Do not stir up or awaken love until the appropriate time" is repeated over and over in this short, beautiful book of love poetry.

> "Do not stir up or awaken love
> until the appropriate time"
> (Song of Solomon 2:7, *HCSV*).

While sex is something to be enjoyed, God's Playbook makes it clear that sex is not to be indulged in with reckless abandon or the live-for-the-moment gratification that our culture teaches. Instead, we are to wait for love within the boundaries of marriage, which is why it's so important to allow our feelings and emotions to remain "asleep."

Most people used to view sex as a private act, created by God for intimacy within a marriage to strengthen both the physical and spiritual aspects of the relationship. But today, sex has been downgraded from a spiritual connection with God and our spouse to a fleeting act of self-satisfaction. If you've ever watched an old black and white movie and compare it to movies made today, you have an idea what I'm talking about. In old movies, men would challenge each other to a duel to protect the reputation and honor of a woman. It was more common to see a gentleman kiss a lady's hand as they said goodnight than to watch two people go at it in a sleazy motel. Rather than being disparaged, purity was viewed with the utmost esteem. Sex was something to be protected and honored, not something to be flaunted.

But times have changed. Sexual intimacy outside of marriage is something that is paraded before us every day. We see it on primetime television, in movies (and not just in R-rated ones), on celebrity news programs, on magazine covers and in books. We see it in the daily lives of the people who surround us at school, at work and in our neighborhoods.

Despite the attitudes and practices of the world around us, God's "do not arouse before it's time" advice has never changed. It is just as important for us today as it was for Solomon, and it's advice we'd be wise to pay attention to. Ecclesiastes 3:1 says, "There is a time for everything, and a season for every activity under heaven." That includes romantic relationships. The consequences of stirring up love before its time are disastrous. Statistics about dating reveal the risks of premature romantic involvement. Would you have guessed that 91 percent of girls who begin dating at age 12 lose their virginity before they graduate from high school? But of girls who wait to date until age 16, only 20 percent lose their virginity before they graduate! Waiting makes a difference.

If you think about it, society expects us to make the biggest decisions of our lives while we're very young and the least equipped to make them. We all want to be in control of our lives, but when it comes to the most important decisions (college, career, life partner, and so on), we often allow our feelings and emotions to take over. I personally don't feel ready to make half the decisions I'm supposed to make! That's one reason I welcome God's advice to wait on love.

I don't know about you, but I would much rather err on the side of caution than chase after love and make a mistake that could haunt me for the rest of my life. I'm cautious about awakening love too soon because I know what can happen if it's the wrong person or the wrong time.

Surrendering to God's Protection

When love is experienced the way God intended, there are no words to describe how amazing it is. (That's what my parents and friends have told me, in addition to God's

CAUTION:
Dating Too Early

Ninety-one percent of girls who begin dating at age 12 lose their virginity before graduation.

Fifty-six percent of girls who begin dating at age 13 lose their virginity before graduation.

Fifty-three percent of girls who begin dating at age 14 lose their virginity before graduation.

Forty percent of girls who begin dating at age 15 lose their virginity before graduation.

Twenty percent of girls who begin dating at age 16 lose their virginity before graduation.[1]

Playbook. I think I can trust them!) Premature love, on the other hand, has a tendency to be selfish and self-centered. Not only that, but stirring up love prematurely creates desires that can't righteously be fulfilled outside of marriage and leads to feelings of possessiveness and jealousy. I think we've all seen jealousy gone awry. You may have found yourself in a relationship with someone who didn't want you to talk to anyone else or who wanted all of your time. Although we're sometimes fooled into thinking that such demonstrations of jealousy are expressions of caring, it usually isn't too long before we see that a jealous partner doesn't have our best interests in mind.

But there's another kind of jealousy that *does* have our best interests in mind and always seeks to protect us: God's jealousy. The idea of a jealous God may surprise you, but God loves us more than we can comprehend and He is jealous for His will to be perfected in us. Second Corinthians 11:2 says, "For I am jealous for you with the jealousy of God himself. I promised you as a pure bride to one husband—Christ."

God is jealous for us because He has promised us to Christ! God knows how easily our minds can be led astray, taking our hearts and bodies with it, and as a loving Father, He wants to prevent that from happening. He wants to guard our hearts so that we can be pure and holy before Christ, but it's our decision whether or not we allow Him to protect us. Let's look to God's Word to learn what it looks like to surrender ourselves to God's protection.

Paul started his letter to the Romans by identifying himself as a "bondservant" of Jesus Christ (see *NKJV*). That may not make a lot of sense to us, but the Romans knew that a bondservant had not been sold into slavery—a bondservant was someone who *willingly* surrendered to the lordship of another. Paul was saying that he willingly gave control of his life to Jesus and that he no longer considered himself to have any rights, except those given to him by God.

> By giving ourselves to God, His will can be perfected in us.

With the idea of the bondservant in mind, Paul went on to challenge us to give our bodies to God as a living and holy sacrifice (see Rom. 12:1-2), refusing to copy the behaviors and customs of the world by allowing God to transform us into new people who think differently. "Then you will learn to know God's will for you, which is good and pleasing and perfect." By giving ourselves to God as bondservants and living sacrifices, His will can be perfected in us.

Mary, the mother of Jesus, also considered herself to be a bondservant of God. When the angel appeared to Mary to tell her that she would give birth to the Messiah, she didn't complain about the possible consequences for herself (such as the social stigma and disgrace of being an unwed mother). Instead, she replied, "I am a bondservant of the Lord; may it be as you have said."[2]

I don't know about you, but I've got a lot to learn about being a bondservant of the Lord! I wish that Mary's words, "Lord, may it be as you have said," would be my first response to a difficult or painful situation. Unfortunately, I'm a selfish person. I'm usually much more concerned with how something will affect me than I am with surrendering to God's will and protection.

We face choices every single day, but at the root of our decisions is a basic choice to yield our will and desires to God or to hold them tightly in our control. First Corinthians 6:12 tells us that while everything is acceptable for us, not everything is beneficial. It is up to us to choose whether or not to allow God to protect us from things that aren't "beneficial."

Surrendering to God's Timing

If we are going to allow God to protect and guard our hearts, we have to be willing to wait for His timing. In her book *Keep a Quiet Heart,* Elisabeth Elliot says, "Waiting requires patience."[3] We must be willing to accept the place God has put us before He will allow us to move on. Patience doesn't come easily, but waiting for God's timing is worth the effort.

We must be willing to accept the place God has put us before He will allow us to move on.

I remember talking with girlfriends when I was little about what we thought it would be like to grow up and have a boyfriend. But as the years passed, I was surprised that once we reached the age when we could date, we didn't really want to. Well, we wanted to, but we knew we weren't ready! We knew it was more important to surrender to God's timing, so we were willing to wait.

It certainly isn't easy. At times we become impatient, but it's amazing to look back at all the guys we could have dated—maybe *would have* dated—and be incredibly thankful we never did! There are so many things we found out by just remaining friends that we might never have found out otherwise. If we had jumped headlong into relationships, we wouldn't have known until it was too late to turn back. And the chances are really good that we would have ended up with broken hearts.

One of my life verses is Psalm 40:5: "Many, O LORD my God, are the wonders you have done. The things you planned for us no one can recount to you; were I to speak and tell of them, they would be too many to declare" (*NIV*). I can't tell you the countless times I have come back to this verse whenever I have felt discouraged or alone. I see this verse as a constant reminder that God has something wonderful planned for me. Rather than being frustrated and discontent with my singleness, I have learned to find satisfaction in Jesus, knowing that He will bring someone into my life when His timing is right. All I have to do is wait for it to unfold!

Waiting Faithfully

One of my all-time favorite songs is "Faithfully" by Eric and Leslie Ludy.[4] It speaks of faithfully waiting for one's future spouse. During the long and lonely nights of singleness, it has often reminded me of what I'm waiting for and the incredible gift I will some day be able to present to my husband: the gift of absolute purity.

I think Psalm 27:14 puts the waiting part of purity in perspective: "Wait patiently for the LORD. Be brave and courageous. Yes, wait patiently for the LORD." It might sound funny to talk about waiting faithfully as being brave and courageous, but it truly is. It's not easy to wait. In fact, I think one of the hardest things God can ever say is "Not now."

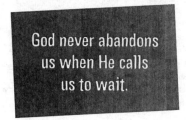

God never abandons us when He calls us to wait.

As difficult as waiting can be, God never abandons us when He calls us to wait. That's why Paul can say in Romans 5:3-5:

We can rejoice, too, when we run into problems and trials, for we know that they help us develop endurance. And endurance develops strength of character, and character strengthens our confident hope of salvation. And this hope will not lead to disappointment. For we know how dearly God loves us, because he has given us the Holy Spirit to fill our hearts with his love.

Psalm 145 says that God is faithful to all of His promises and loving toward all He has made. "You give them their food at the proper time. You open your hand and satisfy the desires of every living thing" (*NIV*). Does this mean that God will always give you what you want? Of course not, but it does mean that if God doesn't give you what you want, it's for a reason—God longs to give good gifts to His children (see Matt. 7:11). There's a time and a season for everything (see Eccles. 3:1-8). God loves you more than you'll ever be able to comprehend, and if your heart is filled with the love of the Holy Spirit, you have everything you need in order to wait faithfully for the right time and season for relationships.

Only Fools Rush In

God has given us everything we need to wait for His perfect will and timing, but sometimes we feel that we just can't wait a moment longer. That's the way it was with Matthew and Tracy. They met at college, and their chemistry was electric from the beginning. It wasn't long before they were engaged. Matthew picked out a ring; Tracy found the perfect wedding dress. Together they decided on a honeymoon location. Everything seemed perfect.

Then real life set in. They started fighting. A lot. As their arguing intensified, they realized there were just too many things wrong with their relationship to consider getting married. They decided to remain friends, but their relationship was complicated. They kept falling back into old patterns of hugging, kissing and cuddling.

For the next three years they had an "on again, off again" relationship. They both dated other people, but always came back to each other—they just didn't feel right with anyone but each other. Tracy says she'll always love Matthew and can't bear the thought of his ever being with anyone else. Matthew says he doesn't know if he could ever be happy with another woman.

Looking back, Matthew and Tracy say they made some huge mistakes in their relationship. They are the first to admit that they didn't make God the focus of their life together. Instead of waiting for God's timing, they rushed into things and it exploded in their faces. Matthew eventually married someone else, while Tracy is still waiting for her Prince Charming. When I asked if there was any advice she would give to young women contemplating a relationship, it's this: "Don't rush into anything. Take the time to pray about it."

God doesn't paint a beautiful sunset in a single day— He spends a long time waiting for just the right atmospheric conditions to fall into place. In the same way, we shouldn't feel the need to rush into anything. God's best really *is* best! He clearly spells out in the Bible the priorities that enable us to wait faithfully for His perfect timing: "Delight yourself in the LORD and he will give you the desires of your heart" (Ps. 37:4, *NIV*). This is not referring to lustful, fleshly desires, but to the wholesome desires that God Himself places within our hearts, including the desire for human companionship. When the time to begin a relationship is right, God will bring everything together and make the picture of His perfect will incredibly clear. While we wait, we delight in the Lord and look forward to His fulfillment of our hearts' deepest longings.

And I am certain that God, who began the good work within you, will continue his work until it is finally finished on the day when Christ Jesus returns (Phil. 1:6).

Notes

1. Josh McDowell and Bob Hostetler, *Josh McDowell's Handbook on Counseling Youth* (Dallas: Word Publishing, 1996), pp. 283-284. Statistics from study of 2,400 teens conducted by Brent Miller of Utah State University and Terrence Olsen of Brigham Young University.
2. The Greek word for "bondservant" used in Luke 1:38 is *doulous*, which is sometimes translated as "servant," "slave," "handmaiden" or "maidservant."
3. Elisabeth Elliot, *Keep a Quiet Heart* (Grand Rapids, MI: Revell Books, 2004).
4. Eric W. and Leslie Ludy, "Faithfully," © Winston and Brooks, Inc., Windsor, Colorado.

Guarding Your Heart on the World Wide Web

Did you ever see the movie *The Net* starring Sandra Bullock? A futuristic suspense thriller, it portrays a woman whose sole contact with the world is through the Internet. She becomes the target of identity theft but is unable to fight it because no one knows what she looks like! In an instant, her driver's license, bank accounts and credit cards vanish, and she's left to put the pieces of her life back together.

The story line might sound a bit extreme, but it's not that far-fetched for some of us. Cyberspace allows total and complete anonymity. We are physically isolated from the rest of the world and yet still connected, which makes it easy for us to live in a fantasy world of our own making.

The problem is, our feelings and emotions don't distinguish between real life and cyberspace. We can become just as emotionally entangled in online attachments as in real life. Even worse, it often happens without our realizing it.

Be honest: Have you ever thought about the effect the Internet has on your emotional, spiritual and sexual purity? Why don't you take the quiz below to see just how involved you are? Circle *Yes* or *No* for each of the following questions.

1. Do you rush home from school to get online?
   Yes/No

2. Do you spend more than an hour online each day?
   Yes/No

3. Do you check your e-mail more than twice a day?
   Yes/No

4. Do you go into withdrawals if you go more than a day without going online?
   Yes/No

5. Do you send more than five e-mails a day to the same person?
   Yes/No

6. Do you talk to strangers online?

   Yes/No

7. Do you play RPGs (Role Playing Games) online?

   Yes/No

8. Do you spend time thinking about what you'd like to be doing online?

   Yes/No

9. Do you visit sites you wouldn't want other people to know about?

   Yes/No

10. Do you bring your computer on vacation so that you can access the Internet?

    Yes/No

11. Do you tell people things online that you wouldn't tell them in person?

    Yes/No

12. Do you wish you were the same person in real life as you are on the Internet?

    Yes/No

If you answered *yes* to three or more of these questions, you need to seriously evaluate if you are using the Internet or if the Internet is using you. The Internet can be a wonderful tool, but it can also destroy us if we're not careful. I want to share with you some simple ways to help guard your heart and protect your purity on the Internet. In the same way that we have a strategy to control our emotions, it is essential to develop a strategy to control our online habits.

Chat Rooms

The number one problem with the Internet is anonymity. In cyberspace you can be anyone you want to be, see anything you want to see and say anything you want to say—all without anyone knowing your identity. The lack of accountability allowed by Internet anonymity is probably at its most dangerous in chat rooms.

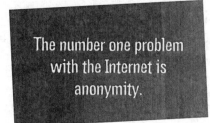

The number one problem with the Internet is anonymity.

There are countless chat rooms available, offering everything from homework helps to faceless hookups (or worse). Personally, I think chat rooms should be avoided at all costs—there's no way to know to whom you're talking! We learned about "stranger danger" when we were kids, but somehow now we think it's okay to talk to strangers online? No way! Even though chat rooms can be entertaining, the risks far outweigh the benefits. Not only are they a huge time waster, they are a creepy haven for emotional entrapment.

On a website called ChatDanger.com, I found a list of safety tips that are meant to protect kids from predators. However, I think the tips are just as applicable to guarding your heart online at any age. If you're going to chat (which I don't recommend), take these practical tips with you!

- *Be careful who you trust online.* Remember that online "friends" are still strangers. People online, no matter how long you have been talking to them or how friendly they are, may not be who they say they are.

- *Remember that meeting someone you have only been in touch with online can be dangerous.* Never agree to meet with someone you met online unless you take a responsible adult with you.

• *Stay in charge while chatting.* Keep your personal information (such as your name, address, telephone number, cell number, private e-mail address and picture) private when chatting online, even if people ask for it. Although it can be tempting to reveal more than you normally would in online friendships, giving out personal information can make you vulnerable and put you in dangerous situations. Also, check your profile and make sure it doesn't include any personal information.

• *Get away from an unpleasant situation in a chat room by logging out.* This just takes one click or can be done by changing your screen name.

• *Think before you answer private messages.* It can be harder to end a conversation in a private chat than in a public chat. A private chat may end up being more personal than you like. If someone doesn't want to talk in a public chat, then you need to be very careful.

- *Use a nickname, not your real name.* Make sure it's a nickname that's not going to attract unwanted attention.

- *Look out for your friends.* Do something if you think that they are in danger.

- *Tell someone if you encounter uncomfortable situations online.* Tell your parent (or a trusted adult) if someone or something makes you feel uncomfortable, worried or scared.[1]

IMing

IMing is another risky Internet activity. When I first got an Instant Messenger on my computer, my parents made a rule that I couldn't be online past 10 P.M. At the time I hated it. I thought it was completely unfair.

"But everyone talks after 10!" I whined. "Most people don't even start talking until then!" But they refused to be swayed.

Looking back, I'm thankful for their foresight. I got into enough trouble talking online during the day! Remember Eric? We IMed for *hours* every day. I'm convinced that we never would have gotten so involved if it hadn't been for one "harmless" little thing: IM. When we weren't chatting online, we were e-mailing back and forth. As a result, we became very comfortable with each other. We said a lot of things we would never have dreamed of saying in person, but because it was online, it felt safe. We didn't realize how vulnerable we were making ourselves.

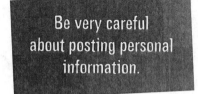

Be very careful about posting personal information.

Virtual Communities

During my first week at college, I was introduced to a whole new world: the World of Facebook. It was pretty much expected that *everyone* had a page on Facebook (or Xanga or MySpace). I jumped in with both feet and didn't think it was a big deal at first, but I'll never forget a message written to me by one of the guys at school: "Don't let Facebook take your life away as it has mine." It didn't take me long to realize just how addicting they can be.

I'm not here to knock Facebook, Xanga or MySpace, but we shouldn't be naïve: It's important to be aware of the dangers that sites like these can pose. We need to take precautions to make sure we're not being led into dangerous waters. The key to using sites like these is to be very careful about posting personal information. Posting personal details online gives others an intimate glimpse into your life that can create an emotional attachment for them that you know nothing about. Such attachments can lead to stalking and other threats or harm. (It works the other way around, too. If you're using these sites to check out all the hotties on campus, then you've probably crossed some boundaries!)

I'll admit that I've been guilty of rushing from class to check Facebook to see whether or not a certain guy is single. While this is seemingly harmless, it can lead to unhealthy fantasies that can lead me in a direction I don't want to go. The bottom line is, unless I'm ready to begin a committed relationship with someone, I don't need to be fantasizing about them—no matter how innocent it might seem.

E-mail

Monitoring your e-mail usage is another aspect of guarding your heart online. When Eric and I were dancing around the issue of a relationship, we sent as many as 20 e-mails in a single day. Not only was it obsessive, but it also created an artificial emotional bond that neither of us knew was there.

If you're e-mailing with a member of the opposite sex, I strongly encourage you to set limits on how many e-mails you send. Be careful what you say. When in doubt, take a breather to pray about it. I now wait at least a day or two before answering most e-mails from guys—not because I don't care or am playing hard to get, but because I know that responding quickly sends a message that I'm really eager to talk. I want to avoid the potential complications of firing off quick e-mails.

If you think you've crossed some boundaries via e-mail, get yourself an e-mail accountability partner. Send that person blind copies of all your e-mails or give him or her free access to your inbox. When someone else is watching, things are less likely to get out of hand.

RPGs (Role-Playing Games)

When it comes to online entrapments, there are few things as dangerous as RPGs. Role-Playing Games are specifically designed to fuel fantasies in the imaginations of the players. The ultimate goal is to create an experience that is different from the real world, a place where players are able to escape the constraints, expectations and pressures of life. (That definitely doesn't sound like a pastime that will help you keep your heart and emotions in check!)

I'm sure there are some fairly harmless RPGs, but on the whole, they are a virtual cesspool of emotional entrapment. They are like an open invitation to let your fantasies and emotions run wild. In addition, it's rare to find an RPG that doesn't have witches, monsters, magic and spells—things that are in direct opposition to a pure, godly, Christian lifestyle. When taken to the extreme, RPGs can become addictive and excessive to the point of being detrimental to your physical and emotional health. (And you'll never get anything else done!)

Online Dating

I remember talking to a girl who had an online romance with a guy from England. A few weeks into it, she realized she was in over her head and needed to end the relationship, but it wasn't easy. As we talked, she started to cry and told me that even though they had only talked online, she felt incredibly close to the guy. She didn't want to hurt him. In just a few weeks, she had already given a part of her heart away and was struggling to get it back.

The problem with online relationships is that it's so much easier to say very intimate things when you're "talking to the screen" than when talking face to face with a real person. This is one reason that so many people meet someone online, spend hours and hours talking and then fly halfway across the country to meet the person—only to find out that the real person is nothing like the online person!

> Online dating fosters a false sense of security that quickly leads into dangerous territory.

This was also true in my relationship with Eric. Believe it or not, we never discussed our relationship in person—that part of our lives remained exclusively online. The attachments we formed online weren't even reflected in real life! Does that sound like emotional purity to you?

I think a good strategy for purity requires us to avoid online dating at all costs. Oh, I've heard arguments like "What's the big deal about meeting someone online? Lots of people have done it and succeeded." While I'm not trying to discount anyone's success story, I strongly believe that online dating fosters a false sense of security that quickly leads into dangerous territory. (Not only that, but there are a lot of weirdos online.)

Internet Porn

We've already explored the implications of sexual promiscuity on our emotions, but what about the online world of pornography? By the way, ladies—don't stop reading. If you think porn is something only guys struggle with, think again. I have several girlfriends who have come to me in tears, admitting they allowed themselves to be sucked into an online fantasy world and couldn't get themselves out.

To keep from falling into these patterns, my accountability partner and I use a program called X3 Watch. X3 Watch is a software program designed to encourage online integrity and purity. Whenever you browse the Internet and access a site that may contain questionable material, the program saves the site name on your computer in a hidden folder. A person of your choice (your accountability partner) then receives an e-mail containing a list of sites generated from that folder. According to the creators of the program, "This information is meant to encourage open and honest conversation between friends and help us all be more accountable."[2]

I'll tell you from personal experience that whenever I've been tempted to visit a site I shouldn't, knowing that someone else would get a report helped me to resist the temptation. Whichever filtering service you choose, I encourage you to install it right away to help keep your thoughts and emotions in check.

Guard Your Time

In order to keep the Internet from controlling you, it's crucial to set time limits as to the amount of time you spend online. We can form unhealthy emotional attachments to the Internet itself, just as we form attachments to people. It can even become an idol that hinders our relationship with God and obstructs our pursuit for His best for our lives.

> An idol is anything that gets more of our attention than God.

It's a bit like the fiction addiction I had in junior high. I read *all* the time—and if I wasn't reading, I was *thinking* about reading. While reading itself isn't bad (obviously),

I had become completely obsessed with escaping into fictional stories about other people's lives. I was making it an idol in my life. (An idol is anything that gets more of our attention than God.)

I'll never forget the day God asked me to fast from reading. "Brienne," He said. "If you really love Me, you'll give up your novels for the next 40 days." I couldn't imagine going that long with out a "fic fix"! At the same time, I knew I needed to show God that He was most important in my life.

After I got past the initial stages of withdrawal, I discovered that there was much more to life than just books. I started spending more time with friends and family, hanging out, watching movies, whatever. I never realized how much I'd been missing out on! I didn't have time for any of those things when I was reading all the time.

If you've realized that the Internet has become an idol in your life, I challenge you to do the same thing I did with books. Make a commitment to fast from the Internet. It may sound extreme, but I guarantee it will help you to take a step back and gain some perspective on your life. Who knows? You may discover that you've given more of your heart away than you intended. Use the time to work on your relationship with God, and when the fast is over you'll have a much better handle on how to guard your heart on the Internet, set some boundaries and reestablish your priorities.

Notes
1. "How to Keep Safe in Chat," Chatdanger.com, Childnet International, 2004. http://www.chatdanger.com/chat/safetyadvice.aspx (accessed February 2007).
2. "What Is X3watch?" X3watch.com. http://x3watch.com/ (accessed February 2007).

Keys to Escaping Emotional Entanglements

"He asked me for a pencil . . . does that mean he likes me?"

"She noticed my car . . . should I ask her out?"

How many times have you found yourself thinking about that special someone and felt your heart start to thunder and your emotions run wild? If you're at all like me, you have a tendency to blow commonplace events way out of proportion, sending your emotions up and down like a yo-yo. During my short "relationship" with Eric, I practically held my breath every time the phone rang. Every time he looked at me, my stomach dropped to my knees. Even though I didn't realize it at the time, I was becoming emotionally entangled.

Emotional entanglement occurs when we allow events, feelings, conversations, hopes, dreams and emotions to get twisted up in a complicated, confusing mass. When we are emotionally entangled in a relationship, we are swept along by our feelings. We quickly lose perspective and our ability to discern what we are doing. We allow our emotions to rule us rather than the other way around.

The helplessness of such an involvement doesn't sound enticing, but the feelings—well, those are a different story! It's easy to be sucked into the excitement of feeling good and become emotionally entangled as a result. The Bible reveals why we're susceptible to emotional entanglements: We lose sight of our first love. Emotional entanglement happens when we seek fulfillment in the things of this world rather than in God.

This is a problem that goes back thousands of years. In the Old Testament, the prophet Jeremiah was referred to as "the weeping prophet" because he so empathized with God's sorrow over Israel's sin—the sin of forsaking their first love and giving their hearts away to other gods (see Jeremiah 2). Over and over again, Israel had to learn that what the world offers cannot satisfy the deepest longings of our hearts.

> Cultivate a heart that is completely focused on God.

The key to escaping emotional entanglement is to cultivate a heart that is completely focused on God. In the

Bible we find both the command to guard our hearts and the secret of how to do so. The first is found in Proverbs 4:23, which tells us to "guard your heart above all else, for it determines the course of your life." Now I realize this is something that is easier said than done, but the secret for doing so is found in Philippians 4:6-8, which says:

> Don't worry about anything; instead, pray about everything. Tell God what you need, and thank him for all he has done. Then you will experience God's peace, which exceeds anything we can understand. His peace will guard your hearts and minds as you live in Christ Jesus. And now, dear brothers and sisters, one final thing. Fix your thoughts on what is true, and honorable, and right, and pure, and lovely, and admirable. Think about things that are excellent and worthy of praise.

If we would follow the simple instructions laid out in these verses, we would never have to experience the pain of emotional entanglement. If you have not already memorized this short passage, I strongly urge you to start now! If we don't have God's Word as our foundation—if we don't know His Playbook—we will be unable to stand firm in our convictions. We will be powerless to enforce a strategy that will prevent the pain of premature intimacy.

Build Relationships on Integrity

What is integrity? It is strict adherence to moral and ethical principles and honesty, or the quality of being undivided in one's thoughts and actions. One of the reasons we get trapped by our emotions is that we aren't honest with ourselves and the other person. Integrity is essential to building relationships that are free from emotional entanglement. Samuel Johnson, an English author, critic and lexicographer in the eighteenth century, wrote, "Integrity without knowledge is weak and useless, and knowledge without integrity is dangerous and dreadful." Just because we know the Playbook doesn't mean we're putting it into practice. We have to implement a strategy!

One reason I'm so careful about building relationships on a solid foundation of friendship before advancing into romance is because as soon as romance enters the picture, we act, talk and even try to look different than normal. Think about it: Aren't most romantic relationships more like a play than real life, with each person trying to impress the other? Dating encourages us to put our

best foot forward—even to the point of becoming someone we aren't—just to impress the person we're with. If
we're honest, we'll admit that doing this lacks integrity.
When we pretend to be someone we're not, we've crossed
a definite boundary line.

I am much more comfortable getting to know a guy
in a group because there are fewer expectations and less
pressure than when on a "date." I don't have to worry if
my hair is perfect or if I should allow a goodnight kiss.
A guy friend of mine agrees. He much prefers spending
time with a girl in a group rather than one on one because
he feels like he can get to know her better: "I can tell if
she's doing something out of the ordinary because her
friends will call her on it."

> Christian integrity requires us
> to put to death whatever
> belongs to our sinful nature.

Integrity in our relationships isn't only about our vis-
ible behavior—it's about our relationship with God as
well. Our culture tells us that if we "feel" like we're in love,

go for it. But in the book of Colossians, Paul tells us that Christians are supposed to be dead to the desires of this world (see Col. 2). Not only that, but Christian integrity requires us to *put to death* whatever belongs to our sinful nature—including sexual immorality, impurity and lust. In other words, we need to put to death our sinful emotions.

If our feelings and emotions are spurring us toward impure actions, integrity requires that we submit them to God. When we find ourselves in a romantic relationship that we know isn't honoring God, we oftentimes refuse to break it off. That breaks the integrity in our relationship with God and opens the door to emotional entanglements.

Act on the Warning Signs

We've all experienced relationships gone awry, and most of us have seen more than a few unhealthy ones. But what do you do when *you* are the one faced with an unhealthy relationship? How can you know when to make the decision to end an emotionally impure relationship? I don't have all the answers, but I can give you a good two-point litmus test:

1. If you feel isolated from your friends, family or God, it's time to admit that the relationship is emotionally entangled.

2. If you're crossing boundary lines or compromising your convictions, it's time to admit that the relationship is not pure.

Is admitting it easy? Of course not! Even King David—who had a heart that longed for God—had a hard time admitting his relationship was impure. When he allowed himself to become emotionally and physically entangled with another man's wife, God had to send the prophet Nathan to the king to publicly point out his sin (see 2 Sam. 11 and 12). When he finally came to his senses, David poured out his lament to God: "For I know my transgressions, and my sin is always before me. Against you, you only, have I sinned and done what is evil in your sight" (Ps. 51:3-4).

But David also knew where he could find healing and forgiveness:

Create in me a pure heart, O God, and renew a steadfast spirit within me. Do not cast me from your presence or take your Holy Spirit from me. Restore to me the joy of your salvation and grant me a willing spirit, to sustain me (vv. 10-12).

Maybe, like David, you've allowed yourself to become emotionally or physically entangled in a relationship and don't know how to escape. If so, I encourage you to humble yourself before God, repent of whatever sins you've committed and allow His forgiveness to cleanse you. God can create a pure heart in you, regardless of your past. Having a pure heart (that is, a heart that is not emotionally entangled) is impossible apart from God, but with God all things are possible (see Matt. 19:26).

Don't Be Afraid to Start Over

We tend to remember the first Americans as some of the greatest people who ever lived, yet many early Americans were Europe's "undesirables," those who were considered the outcasts of society. These men and women, who were regarded as nobodies in their countries, realized they had a chance for something very special: the chance to start over. They didn't take that opportunity lightly. When they came to America, they made some very strict rules (with even stricter consequences) to ensure they didn't slip back into old patterns. They realized that they were as good as dead if they continued to follow the ways of the world by gratifying the cravings of their sinful natures.

You may think it's too late for you because you've already given your heart away. Maybe you think you are hopelessly caught up in an emotionally entangled relationship. Don't give up! You're not the first one to be in that place, and you certainly won't be the last.

> When we accept God's forgiveness, His grace is all we need.

In her *Lineage of Grace* series of novellas, Francine Rivers follows the lives of five women in the genealogy of Christ. Four of these women had less-than-pure pasts. Tamar was forced into a loveless marriage and became pregnant with her father-in-law's baby; Rahab was a prostitute; Ruth was a pagan outcast; Bathsheba was an adulteress. These four women were linked by sin, but they were also saved by God's grace, His *unmerited favor*. Just picture for a moment the God of the universe reaching down from heaven to embrace you—that's what grace is. None of us deserve God's grace. Romans 3:23 tells us that "all have sinned and fall short of the glory of God." But when we accept God's forgiveness, His grace—unmerited favor—is all we need (see 2 Cor. 12:9).

Maybe you're reading this today and want to reclaim your emotions but feel that your past has left you tainted and dirty. If so, I challenge you to let this be the moment when you take the first step toward reconciliation with God. Decide who the keeper of your heart is and make the decision to start over. You don't have to be defined by your past, because Jesus came to make all things new:

Anyone who belongs to Christ has become a new person. The old life is gone; a new life has begun! (2 Cor. 5:17).

The consequences of emotional entanglements are often very painful, but they are not irreversible. In Psalm 25:7, David begged the Lord, "Do not remember the rebellious sins of my youth. Remember me in the light of your unfailing love, for you are merciful, O LORD." God is always willing to forgive and wipe away our guilt. That's why in Psalm 32:1-2, David rejoiced, "Oh, what joy for those whose disobedience is forgiven, whose sin is put out of sight! Yes, what joy for those whose record the LORD has cleared of guilt, whose lives are lived in complete honesty!"

The key to starting over is just that: letting God wipe your slate clean and starting over. It may require making drastic changes so that you won't fall back into old habits. It may mean breaking off relationships, throwing away computers, finding an accountability partner or revitalizing your prayer life. Whatever your weaknesses are—emotional entanglement, fantasies, masturbation, pornography, sexual permissiveness—the key is to ask God to take control of that area of your life and do whatever is necessary to keep it from controlling you.

> God is always willing to forgive and wipe away our guilt.

My friend Sarah is a powerful reminder to me of the grace and hope God offers us when we start over. Sarah had endured a lifetime of heartache and pain. Her parents divorced when she was very young and she was shuffled back and forth between their homes. Although she was a beautiful girl, her self-esteem was lower than dirt. When she was 13 she became sexually active. She began a destructive cycle of moving from one emotionally entangled relationship to another, desperately trying to find happiness and fill the gnawing emptiness inside her.

When she was 16, she moved in with her boyfriend. She was so emotionally entangled that she endured an abusive relationship for three years. To all who knew her, she seemed to have chosen a one-way ticket to destruction, but at 19, the course of her life changed. She met Jesus and discovered true love for the first time. She realized that she had been looking for intimacy and love in temporary physical and emotional relationships instead of in an eternal relationship with the God of the Universe.

Sarah realized her life was a mess and that she couldn't get it straightened out alone. But she took the first steps: She left her boyfriend, moved back home and started going to church with her family. It wasn't easy. She had a lot of bad habits to break. But she knew God had forgiven her past, and she was determined to follow Christ no matter the cost.

I was with Sarah the day she was baptized into the family of Christ. I listened as she told her testimony of how she had been made brand new by the cleansing power of Jesus to a congregation of nearly 2,000 people. Today Sarah has made a commitment to abstain from drugs, alcohol and sex. "If I told any of my former friends that I was waiting for marriage, they would laugh at me, but I'm a new creation through Jesus. I've been cleansed by the blood of Christ, and I am starting over."

Sarah's story breaks my heart and fills me with joy. No one should have to experience what she went through, but her story serves as an awesome reminder of what Jesus' love can do. If you are reading this today and have blown it in the area of sexual or emotional purity, do not give up. If you feel hopelessly entangled in a relationship, you can start over. God is in the business of forgiveness and restoration. No matter what your past, you can make the decision to live in purity from this day forward!

So you also should consider yourselves to be dead to the power of sin and alive to God through Christ Jesus. Do not let sin control the way you live; do not give in to sinful desires. Do not let any part of your body become an instrument of evil to serve sin. Instead, give yourselves completely to God, for you were dead, but now you have new life. So use your whole body as an instrument to do what is right for the glory of God. Sin is no longer your master, for you no longer live under the requirements of the law. Instead, you live under the freedom of God's grace (Rom. 6:11-14).

Finding Your First Love

A long-time friend of mine recently called me in tears, begging me to *ple-e-e-ease* find her a boyfriend.

"I don't care who he is," she said. "I just can't stand being alone anymore!"

I'm afraid that's the attitude many of us have. Unfortunately, it leads us to rush into relationships because we're afraid of being alone, rather than allowing God to fill our emptiness.

God knows the longings in our hearts because He put them there in the first place. Not only that, He created us with needs and desires that only He can fill. Feeling lonely, discontent or incomplete is not a result of being single—it's a result of not being full of Christ! If you're looking for a person to fulfill your desire for intimacy, you are in for a huge disappointment.

But there *is* a love that can satisfy us. The psalmist writes of it in Psalm 73:28: "But as for me, how good it is to be near God!" If you have not yet discovered how good it is to be near Him, I urge you to work toward falling in love with your heavenly Love before you worry about finding an earthly one.

I know what it's like to want a relationship so bad it physically hurts. I've experienced more than my share of lonely days and long nights, but I've decided that I want a relationship with God more than any other. Sure, I still desire human companionship, but I'm content enough in my relationship with the Lord that I'm fully enjoying my singleness.

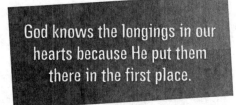

God knows the longings in our hearts because He put them there in the first place.

The bottom line is that God doesn't want us to go through an endless cycle of failed relationships, broken hearts and shattered dreams. We are precious to Him and He longs to fulfill our dreams, but in order to do that we must treasure and guard our purity as He does. In order to have what we desire most, we must be willing to surrender our dreams and desires to the One who created them in the first place.

Call me sentimental, but there's a little thing that has helped me focus on God as my first love and hold fast to His plan for my life when I'm tempted to weaken in the area of guarding my heart. For my seventeenth birthday, I found a really cool necklace: It's a silver lock with a little key attached to it. I decided that necklace would be a reminder to me that God holds the key to my heart and that I'm not giving it to anyone without His permission. Whenever it's hard to maintain my commitments, I wear that necklace as a symbol of my promise to God (and my future husband) that I will continue to guard my heart regardless of the cost.

A necklace may not be your thing, but I encourage you to find something that can serve as a symbol of your commitment to purity. Some of you may have been involved with the *True Love Waits* movement and may have signed a pledge card or may wear a "purity" ring. While those things are great, I want to challenge you to take that commitment one step further by promising God that you will guard your heart in the same way you have pledged to guard your body. Maybe you could write a promise to God in the front of your Bible, or create a contract with God and carry it in your wallet. Or maybe you need to have a ceremony where you pledge to remain pure physically, spiritually *and* emotionally. Whatever you do, make sure that you have something *tangible* that can remind you of your commitments—because when the rubber meets the road, good intentions don't cut it! As fallible human beings, we sometimes need something we can touch in order to be reminded of our commitments.

Growing Deeper in Love with Our First Love

Our relationship with God is established by our confession of sin and His offer of forgiveness. But though the relationship is established, it will continue to change as long as we live—if we want to discover the full joy and satisfaction to be found in a deep connection with God, we have to invest in that relationship.

Can you honestly say that you're putting as much time and energy into your relationship with Christ as you are (or would be) into a romantic relationship? If not, your romantic relationship is not what God intends for you. Until you are satisfied with the fullness of Christ, you will never be fully satisfied in a human relationship.

It may seem strange to think of having an intimate love relationship with the God of the universe, but once you experience love the way God intended it, you'll never be satisfied with anything else. And the good news is that getting started in this relationship is only a prayer away!

I'll never forget the day I discovered how important prayer is in my relationship with God. It was springtime and my family and I were ministering in the Hawaiian Islands. As we explored, I noticed that all the Catholic churches advertised daily Mass. Going to church every day is a foreign concept to most of us, but it reminded me of Acts 2:42, where "all the believers devoted themselves *daily* to the apostles' teaching, and to fellowship, and to sharing in meals (including the Lord's Supper), and to prayer." The chapter goes on to tell about miracles and wonders and how "each day the Lord added to their fellowship those who were being saved" (v. 47). I realized that the Early Christians had something I wanted—daily fellowship and connection with their first love! I longed to be as connected with God as the Early Christians, and to share daily in what God is doing in the world!

I realized that if I wanted to experience the kind of connection the Early Christians had with their first love, I had to be willing to spend serious time in daily prayer with other believers. I asked the Lord to bring along like-minded people who would join with me for a time of daily intercessory prayer. By the time we got back from that trip, God had lined up three other people who shared my same passion and vision! We started meeting together every day from 6:00 until 7:00 A.M. but soon discovered that wasn't long enough. We extended our prayer time to an hour and a half, then to two hours and finally to two and a half hours every morning. At first it was difficult, but I found that the more I prayed, the more I *wanted* to pray. Everything else in life paled in comparison to spending time with Jesus.

An extended daily prayer time may not seem doable to you, but I want to encourage you to set aside a portion of each day to sit in the presence of God. My morning prayer time has become the most precious part of my day—it's the part of my day when I spend quality time with my first love. And no matter how much stuff I have to do, I've discovered that if I give God the first part of my day, everything else falls into place. Jesus promises that if we seek after Him (that is, *pray*) and live righteously, He will give us everything we need (see Matt. 6:33). As one of my professors says, "Prayer is not how we seek for a strategy; prayer *is* our strategy." It's impossible to overestimate the importance of prayer, and it's imperative that we remember how crucial prayer is to every single aspect of our strategy for purity.

Discovering How Much God Loves You

I know it may be a little awkward to think of God as your first love. But the fact is, no one can ever love you as much as your heavenly Father does. God's love for you is unconditional. He loves you exactly the way you are and He wants you to see yourself as His precious child. To Him you are a precious jewel and a rare gem (yes, guys too!). You are the apple of God's eye.

> No one can ever love you as much as your heavenly Father does!

I understand that for some of you, thinking of God in this way is next to impossible. Maybe someone has harmed you and made you feel worthless and unlovable. Maybe you've been hurt so bad you don't even know what it feels like to be loved. My mother struggled with this. She grew up with a very abusive father, so her image of her heavenly Father was very distorted. When she became a Christian, she simply couldn't grasp the concept of a loving Father who wanted to protect her and guard her heart. Her entire way of thinking had to be retrained—she did that by immersing herself in God's Word, meditating on it until the principles were transferred from her head to her heart. She had to follow the same advice she later gave me: Believe what you *know* is true about God, not what you *feel* is true about God.

From the time I was a little girl, I can remember hearing Mom repeat a song called "The Father's Song" by Jamie Owens that she had memorized because it helped her learn how deeply God loved her. It reminded her how much He wanted to protect her from pain: "How many times I have longed to hold you and protect you from the pain the world can give. But you run, every time I get near you. Can't you see, I want to teach you how to live?"[1]

This is how God, our loving Father, sees us, His children. He weeps with those who weep. He mourns with those who mourn. He is a Father to the fatherless and a Friend to the friendless. But so often we push Him aside, determined to do it on our own when He longs for us to reach out to Him for protection. Listen to His loving heart in Proverbs 23:26: "O my son, give me your heart. May your eyes take delight in following my ways." God begs for us to give Him our hearts—not so that He can control us, but so that He can protect us.

God wants you to live a pure life and have a pure heart because He wants the very best for you! He sent His only Son, Jesus, to make that possible. As Jesus died on the cross and said, "It is finished," He broke the chains of impurity that try to keep us prisoner. Not only that, He promised to send a helper, the Holy Spirit, who comes to guide us every step of the way. But it's up to us whether or not we will reach out and take hold of the promises He's given us and the Helper He has sent.

Committing Yourself to Your First Love

From the time I first made a commitment to purity when I was 13, I begged God to keep my emotions in check, to hold on to my heart and to help me find complete contentment and satisfaction in Him. I'm convinced that God's help is the only reason I realized what was happening in my relationship with Eric. Thankfully, the Holy Spirit's guidance made it possible for me to stop going in the wrong direction and get back on the right track.

What about you? Are you reaching out and making use of the help God's given you? God longs to be the love of your life—in fact, He created you because He wanted to be in fellowship with you! But the question is, will you guard your heart and hold on to your emotions? Or will you turn away, determined to do it on your own?

> Are you ready to make God the first love of your life?

It is my hope that God has been convicting you of the areas in your life where you have been less than pure. Remember, He wants what's best for you. He wants you to have clean, pure, loving relationships—not muddy, painful, messy ones. But the only way to do that is to give your heart *completely* to Christ and build your love relationship with Him *before* you try to build a human love relationship. Then, and only then, will you find the satisfaction, contentment and fulfillment you long for. Today I want to challenge you to start falling in love with your "Heavenly Fiancé," because when you do, your eyes will be opened to a deeper love than you ever knew existed! [2]

Teach me your way, O LORD, and I will walk in your truth; give me an undivided heart, that I may fear your name (Ps. 86:11).

Notes

1. Jamie Owens, "The Father's Song," © 1975 Bud John/EMI Christian Group.
2. I borrowed this image from Debby Jones and Jackie Kendall's book *Lady in Waiting* (Orlando, FL: Destiny Image Publishers, 2005).

Life with No Regrets

As a young woman who is waiting for God to bring the right man into my life, I have come to the realization that singleness is a precious gift from God. I certainly don't want to be single forever, but I believe that I'm in the center of God's will for this time in my life. While I'm single, I don't have the distractions that a married person has, so I can focus completely on God and the tasks He has for me right now.

At the beginning of 2005, during my evening devotions, I felt God ask me a very difficult question.

Brienne, He said. *Are you prepared to be single for seven more years?*

Part of me didn't want to answer, but God had already taught me the value of giving everything over to Him, so I reluctantly said yes. Immediately I was reminded of what I had read in my Bible that morning: "So Jacob worked seven years for Rachel. But it only seemed like a few days, he loved her so much" (Gen. 29:20). I felt that God was asking me to be willing to give Him the next seven years of my life in complete service to Him. Just as previously God had tested my willingness to give up my future plans, He was now testing my love for and commitment to Him. Was I willing to sacrifice my timetable for a romantic relationship?

Now I don't know that it will be that long until God brings someone into my life, but I do know that God asked if I would be *willing* to wait. Until then, I can focus 100 percent of my time, talent and treasure on serving God and fulfilling His plans for my life. And though it's difficult to think of being single for that long, it's also freeing to realize that I don't have to worry about finding Mr. Right. When the time comes, God will bring him to me. And just as He had promised me He would write me a more incredible love story than I could ever imagine, He also promised that whatever I gave over to Him, He would turn into something better than I could ever plan. As difficult as it was, I'm so glad I did—when I look back at my plans for my life, they pale in comparison to what God has done.

In my limited understanding of what God wanted for my life, I had tried to figure everything out on my own. But God's ways are not our ways. I never dreamed that I would write this book, travel around the world sharing in music ministry, earn two undergraduate degrees in the time it would normally take to earn one, or be a music editor for a major Christian newspaper. God's plans for my life are so much bigger than I ever imagined, and had I not given control over to Him, I never would have experienced all the blessings He had in store for me.

I'll be the first to say that giving control over to God was terrifying in the beginning, but I can also say it's more than worth it. I can't guarantee what will happen if you give control of your life over to God, but I do know that He loves you more than you could ever imagine and that He has a plan for your life that is far better than anything you could ever come up with (see Ps. 40:5). It's been a long journey, but like the prophet Isaiah, I can now say:

> I am overwhelmed with joy in the LORD my God!
> For he has dressed me with the clothing of salvation and draped me in a robe of righteousness.
> I am like a bridegroom in his wedding suit or a bride with her jewels (Isa. 61:10).

This joy can be experienced by all of us who make Jesus our first love. We (the Church) are Christ's bride, and it's our job to make sure that we're watching and waiting for Him. It's just like the parable that Jesus told about the 10 virgins:

Then the Kingdom of Heaven will be like ten bridesmaids who took their lamps and went to meet the bridegroom. Five of them were foolish, and five were wise. The five who were foolish didn't take enough olive oil for their lamps, but the other five were wise enough to take along extra oil. When the bridegroom was delayed, they all became drowsy and fell asleep.

At midnight they were roused by the shout, "Look, the bridegroom is coming! Come out and meet him!"

All the bridesmaids got up and prepared their lamps. Then the five foolish ones asked the others, "Please give us some of your oil because our lamps are going out."

But the others replied, "We don't have enough for all of us. Go to a shop and buy some for yourselves."

But while they were gone to buy oil, the bridegroom came. Then those who were ready went in with him to the marriage feast, and the door was locked.

Later, when the other five bridesmaids returned, they stood outside, calling, "Lord! Lord! Open the door for us!"

But he called back, "Believe me, I don't know you!"

So you, too, must keep watch! For you do not know the day or hour of my return (Matt. 25:1-13).

Just as the 10 virgins didn't know when the bridegroom would come for his bride, we don't know when God will bring our future mate into our life. It's our job to make sure that we're content and complete in our relationship with Jesus so that we're ready for a human relationship when God sees fit to bring it.

What about you? Are you living like the wise virgins or the foolish ones? Is your life focused on becoming the person God wants you to be and falling in love with your Heavenly Fiancé, or are you distracted by the things of this world, chasing after things that are empty and unsatisfying? Until you passionately seek after your first love, the time will never be right for an earthly love.

Is It Time for Love?

You're probably wondering how you can tell when the time is right for an earthly love. Just how do we differentiate between an emotional entanglement and a pure love relationship? It would be much easier if God just gave us a relationship manual with all the rules perfectly spelled out—unfortunately, there's no one-size-fits-all answer! But I can give you some keys that will help you determine when the time is right to begin a pure and God-honoring relationship:

1. Are you spending time with God on a daily basis?
2. Do you have a list of what you're looking for in a life partner?
3. Do you have a list of things you will and will not do in a relationship?
4. Do you have clearance from God (and the authorities He's put in your life such as your parents, pastor or mentor) about proceeding in a relationship?

While this is certainly not an exhaustive list, keeping these things in mind will help you to steer clear of the pitfalls of the casual dating scene and avoid falling for a counterfeit of the true love God intends for you.

The world tells us that love is a feeling, but the Bible tells us something very different. Remember the definition of love from 1 Corinthians 13:4-7?

Love is patient and kind. Love is not jealous or boastful or proud or rude. It does not demand its own way. It is not irritable, and it keeps no record of being wronged. It does not rejoice about injustice but rejoices whenever the truth wins out. Love never gives up, never loses faith, is always hopeful, and endures through every circumstance.

If you have a relationship that matches up to these criteria, then you're experiencing love the way God designed it. But if your relationship does not measure up, I challenge you to do some serious soul searching.

> "Love never gives up,
> never loses faith,
> is always hopeful,
> and endures through
> every circumstance"
> (1 Cor. 13:7).

When I'm old and gray and look back on my "dating career," I don't want to wish I had done things differently.

I want to be able to look back and know that I was in the center of God's perfect plan for my life. I don't want to get to heaven and have to give an account to God for every piece of my heart that I gave away prematurely. I would much rather hold out for a relationship built on true love than waste my time on a cheap imitation! In fact, the most romantic love stories I've ever heard aren't built on romance, but on friendship.

Finding the Love of a Lifetime

Consider for example the amazing friendship of Judy and Justin. Judy grew up in a non-Christian home, but through a strange series of events, visited a Charismatic church. While there, she met a cute blond girl who invited her to a Bible study. Judy was so taken with the girl's sweetness and outgoing personality that she agreed to come. At the Bible study, Judy was introduced to the girl's older brother, Justin, and they hit it off immediately.

Over the next several years, Judy became quite active in the church and felt that God was calling her to be a single missionary. The only problem was, she and Justin had become very close friends and she knew their relationship could turn into something much deeper. But Judy knew that her calling from God was more important than her feelings, so she decided to sever her ties with Justin and move to the mission field.

About that time, Justin started attending seminary in preparation to become a pastor. He met and started dating someone else, but he couldn't get Judy out of his mind. Finally, one night he felt God tell him that he was going to marry Judy. "But Lord," he said, "I don't even know where she is. We haven't spoken in years."

"Trust Me," was all God said.

Meanwhile, four years had passed since Judy had moved to Africa and she was getting ready to come home for a year. One night she awoke to an audible voice: "Judy," God said, "I want you to return home and marry Justin."

"I absolutely will not," she said and promptly went back to sleep.

When the same thing happened the next night, she responded the same way. When it happened the third night, she said, "Lord, this is like when You spoke to Samuel isn't it? I'm listening now. I'll go home, but I'm not going to do anything to make this happen. It's going to have to be all You."

After returning home, Judy was asked to oversee a Bible study for several hundred students at an academy near her church. Because she was a single woman, the pastor asked her to find a male counterpart to work with. "We don't want the young men thinking that only women can teach the Bible," the pastor told her.

"Who do you suggest work with me?" she asked.

"I think you should call your friend Justin," the pastor told her.

Judy couldn't believe her ears! She wrote a very short note to Justin informing him of the academy's need and asking him if he would be willing to come. Needless to say, Justin was shocked to receive Judy's note. "But, Lord," he said, "I don't have a car to get there and even if I did, I don't have a job."

God was obviously working, because less than a week later an elderly lady at his church asked him if he would be willing to drive her back to Illinois to visit her family. "I just don't want to drive that far by myself," she said.

Not long after, Justin's father called to tell him that his old church in Illinois was looking for a youth pastor. "I know you're settled where you are, but we could really use you down here." Everything was falling into place, so Justin made the necessary arrangements to move back to Illinois and begin teaching with Judy.

This started a two-year working relationship between Judy and Justin. It didn't take long for them to renew the close friendship they had once shared, but Judy was determined not to say or do anything that Justin could possibly misinterpret as anything other than friendship. As far as he was concerned, she was still committed to being a single missionary. One night, as Justin poured out his heart to God, he clearly heard the Lord tell him the time was right to propose to Judy.

Without waiting for any further confirmation, he called Judy and asked her if she would be willing to meet him the next morning for a sunrise date on the beach. Judy was surprised, but agreed. Justin didn't sleep a wink that night. Instead, he spent the whole time composing a poem for Judy, telling her how much she meant to him and asking her if she would marry him. Up to this point, they had remained strictly friends, but Justin knew he had heard from God, so he was willing to step out in faith and trust God with his heart.

Judy and Justin have been married for more than 50 years! They are still as much in love today as they were when they got married. I believe their happiness is due to the fact that they were willing to wait for God's perfect timing rather than taking matters into their own hands.

What Kind of Love Do You Want?

The fiery passion of a relationship may fade, but a friendship can last forever. When God finally does bring someone into my life, I don't want to just have a lover— I want to marry my best friend. I want to know that he loves me no matter what—in spite of the times my breath smells, or I wake up with bed-head or I am less-than-pleasant company. I don't want to have to worry about impressing him. I want someone who will be my partner in everything, someone with whom I will be able to share my happiness and sorrow, health and sickness, prosperity and pain.

God may not have given us a relationship manual, but He has given us guidelines in His Word. He wants us to live free from past hurts, disappointments and emotional scars, but those of us who ride the dating roller coaster put our hearts on the line time and time again and lose another little piece every time another relationship ends. Broken hearts cause us to trust less and less, and can leave us feeling used and discarded. If we choose to guard our hearts and remain both physically and emotionally pure, we save ourselves the pain of broken relationships, which sets us free to enter future relationships with no regrets.

> There are consequences to our actions. The good news is, they don't have to be bad!

Regardless of what we want to believe, we can't "live for the moment." There are future consequences to our actions. The good news is, those consequences don't have to be bad. Whether we're dating, courting or waiting on God, it's critically important that we decide how we will approach romantic relationships *before* we find ourselves crossing a line we never meant to cross. When we live as if today affects tomorrow, it helps prevent us from carrying excess baggage into future relationships. Realizing that the choices and decisions we make today directly affect the rest of our lives can save us from a lifetime of regret.

Run with Endurance

God isn't looking for people who are perfect. He's looking for men and women who will believe what He has said and are willing to listen and obey! Just look back on some of the examples we have in the Bible: Saul was a teenager and from the smallest tribe of Israel when God chose him to be king (see 1 Sam. 9); David was a lowly shepherd when he killed the giant Goliath and rescued the Israelites from the Philistines (see 1 Sam. 17); and Solomon was "like a little child" when he was made king of Israel (see 1 Kings 3:7).

I find it interesting that even though each of these individuals struggled to live completely pure lives, they didn't let their past define their future. When their affections wandered, they repented and returned to their first love. The same goes for us. If we want to be known as mighty men and women of God, then we too must follow the words of Hebrews 12:1-2, which says:

Therefore, since we are surrounded by such a huge crowd of witnesses to the life of faith, let us strip off every weight that slows us down, especially the sin that so easily trips us up. And let us run with endurance the race God has set before us. We do this by keeping our eyes on Jesus, the champion who initiates and perfects our faith.

The bottom line is, if we want to live pure lives with no regrets, then we have to be willing to get rid of anything and everything that is slowing us down, regardless of what it costs us.

Living a pure and righteous life doesn't happen by accident. It takes a decision to be purposeful and diligent about our thoughts, words and actions. Personally, my goal is to model my life after Colossians 2:2, which says:

> My purpose is that they [the Body of Christ] may be encouraged in heart and united in love, so that they may have the full riches of complete understanding, in order that they may know the mystery of God, namely, Christ (*NIV*).

What about you? Is there something in your life that is slowing you down and keeping you from running the race that God has laid out for you? Maybe you've allowed yourself to get so caught up in things of this world that, like the believers in Colossi, you've been led astray on some wild-goose chase, chasing after the "secrets" the world has to offer. Maybe you've been giving pieces of your heart away little by little. Maybe you're in a relationship that is tearing you down. Maybe you're practicing physical purity but are engaged in emotional promiscuity without even realizing it. Whatever is keeping you from living in complete purity,

I challenge you to get rid of it and take whatever steps are necessary to keep it from coming back!

Remember, true purity is more than sexual abstinence—it's a commitment, a promise and a choice to guard your heart. Don't let the words of Jesus apply to you: "You are like a whitewashed tomb, which looks beautiful on the outside but on the inside is full of dead men's bones and everything unclean" (Matt. 23:27). True purity means being completely pure in your thoughts, actions, words and emotions.

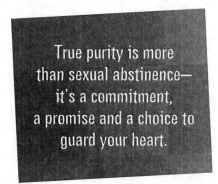

True purity is more than sexual abstinence—it's a commitment, a promise and a choice to guard your heart.

It is my prayer that this book has given you all the tools you need to walk into future relationships with your *eyes wide open*. But the next step is up to you! Are you willing to step up to the plate and make the commitment to true purity? I'm not talking about signing a pledge or wearing a WWJD bracelet—I'm talking about a radical heart change, a decision to completely sell out to your first love, Jesus Christ!

If you take only one thing away from reading this book, I hope it's the decision to live a life of no regrets, steering clear of the emotional roller coaster and avoiding the heartbreak of emotional promiscuity. Remember:

Trust in the LORD with all your heart; do not depend on your own understanding. Seek his will in all you do, and he will show you which path to take (Prov. 3:5-6).

Keeping Our Eyes Open

Questions We Can Ask Ourselves to Avoid the Trap of Emotional Promiscuity and to Stay Pure at Heart

Now that you've read the book, it's time to think about your own story of emotional purity—what has happened in your past, how you are living today, and what you want in your future relationships. The following questions will help you assess where you have been, make necessary corrections and set a path for where you want to be. Remember, emotional purity is up to you—no one else gets to write the story for you, so make sure you live the best life God created you to live.

1. As you read this book, what weaknesses or gaps did you discover in your efforts to guard your heart and live a pure life before God?

2. To what extent do the movies you watch, the friends you hang out with, the words you say, the places you go, the games you play and the Internet sites you visit support your commitment to live a pure life?

3. In what ways have you (perhaps without even knowing it) fallen for a counterfeit when it comes to love? What did you (at least at that time) believe true love to be? On the basis of what you have learned about emotional purity and God's view of love, write down what you now believe true love to be.

4. If you have experienced the pain of a broken heart as a result of being emotionally involved in a relationship, what was the hardest part for you? What do you think made it so difficult? What valuable part of yourself did you give away or lose in that relationship?

5. What consequences have you faced because you gave part of yourself away to someone who was unworthy? What boundaries can you put in place to prevent that from happening again?

6. Whenever we let our feelings run our emotions, we're headed for trouble. To what extent are you allowing your feelings and emotions to control your actions? In which specific areas do you struggle to live according to the truth rather than by your feelings?

7. How have you handled these challenges in the past? What changes do you need to make to actually take control of your emotions and live by what you believe instead of by what you feel? Make a list of the things you've allowed to control and manipulate you and ask God to help you rise above your feelings.

8. If you've been entangled in a web of emotional promiscuity, what does it mean to you that your sinful passions and desires have been crucified with Christ (see Gal. 2:24)?

9. What areas in your life are keeping you from living in true purity (for example, emotional entanglements, fantasies, pornography, sexual permissiveness)? What is your personal boundary list (specific dos and don'ts) for achieving or maintaining purity in each of these areas?

10. Why are each of these boundaries important to you? What does each one help you to protect? Who is your accountability partner to help you guard your heart in these areas? Commit each of these areas to God and ask Him to help you guard your heart in each one.

11. From this day forward, what commitment to living a pure life are you willing to make? Write it down! Be specific

about your commitment. For example, a commitment to purity may involve a commitment to God, a commitment to yourself and a commitment to your future spouse. Write down a specific purity commitment for all three.

12. What changes must you make to live out your commitment to purity from this day forward? What are your personal warning signs that you are headed for trouble in your commitment to emotional purity?

13. Just how strong a hold does the Internet have on your emotional purity? Did you take the test on pages 127-128? If so, were you surprised by the results? What are you going to do?

14. If any aspect of the Internet has become an idol in your life, it may take a concerted effort to make appropriate and necessary changes. What do you need to change? How hard will it be to change? (Be honest with yourself.) What is your strategy for making the change?

15. Take a few minutes to think about the impact your past and present relationships have had on your rela-

tionship with God. Can you honestly say that God has remained in His rightful place, or have your human relationships been a distraction to your relationship with Him? What must you do to put God back (and keep Him) in His rightful place in your heart and life?

16. In what ways does surrendering your relationships and your desires to God make it easier to wait faithfully and patiently for God to bring about His best in your life?

17. What's most difficult for you about giving God this much control over your life? In which areas do you need God's help the most? Who do you know who can stand by you, pray with you and encourage you to be faithful to God's leading in your relationships?

18. Which practical keys to guarding your heart seem like important ones for you to remember? Which ones surprised you? Which key for guarding your heart is the most difficult or challenging for you to practice?

19. Which Scripture passage best reminds you to guard your heart and helps you do it? Write it out:

Now, memorize this passage so that it will always be available to you when you need extra strength to keep your commitment to emotional purity.

Other Books You Might Want to Read

General

Chapman, Gary. *The Five Love Languages of Teenagers.* Chicago, IL: North-field Publishing, 2000.

Garth, Lakita. *The Naked Truth.* Ventura, CA: Regal Books, 2007.

Hostetler, Bob, and Josh McDowell. *Right from Wrong.* Nashville, TN: W Publishing Group, 1994.

Luce, Ron. *It's Only a Tattoo and Other Myths Teens Believe.* Colorado Springs, CO: Cook Communications, 2006.

Ludy, Eric and Leslie. *When God Writes Your Love Story.* Sisters, OR: Multnomah, 2004.

Omartian, Stormie. *The Power of a Praying Teen.* Eugene, OR: Harvest House Publishers, 2005.

St. James, Rebecca. *Wait for Me.* Nashville, TN: Nelson Books, 2006.

Girls Only

Courtney, Vicki. *Between: A Girl's Guide to Life.* Nashville, TN: B&H Publishing Group, 2006.

DiMarco, Haley. *Sexy Girls: How Hot Is Too Hot?* Grand Rapids, MI: Revell, 2006.

Ethridge, Shannon, and Stephen Arterburn. *Every Young Woman's Battle.* Colorado Springs, CO: WaterBrook Press, 2004.

Jones, Debby, and Jackie Kendall. *Lady in Waiting.* Shippensburg, PA: Destiny Image Publishers, 2005.

Ludy, Leslie. *Authentic Beauty.* Sisters, OR: Multnomah, 2007.

Redman, Beth. *Soul Sister.* Ventura, CA: Regal Books, 2004.

Shirer, Priscilla. *A Jewel in His Crown.* Chicago, IL: Moody Publishers, 2004.

Guys Only

Ludy, Eric. *God's Gift to Women.* Sisters, OR: Multnomah, 2003.

Stoeker, Fred, Mike Yorkey and Stephen Arterburn. *Every Young Man's Battle.* Colorado Springs, CO: WaterBrook Press, 2002.

Acknowledgments

First and foremost, I offer all praise and honor to my heavenly Father who inspired me with the idea for this book in the first place. Every good and perfect gift truly comes from above.

To my parents—thank you for filling me with a desire for purity from a young age and modeling it in your relationship with each other.

To my sister—thank you for being my cheerleader and always believing in me!

To my friends and family—thank you for your love and support as I've worked through this process, especially those of you who have offered your advice, suggestions and critiques.

To my editor, Steve—thank you for believing in me enough to take a chance and for pushing me to make this book the best it could be.

To my writing mentor, Amanda—words cannot express everything you have taught me. I couldn't have done this without you!

About the Author

Brienne Murk is the seventh generation in her family in full-time ministry. She currently travels with her family's music group, Myrrh, performing and speaking at churches, camps, conferences, conventions and crusades. Together with her sister Heather, she has developed a youth seminar that focuses on living your faith out loud in the real world. Now in her early twenties, Brienne is also a full-time student and plans to pursue graduate degrees in both journalism and law. Additionally, she has published works in various magazines and newspapers. Her writing and speaking credits include numerous appearances on nationwide and international TV and radio programs. She has also produced a nationally syndicated radio special and a four-part teaching CD series; performed for, produced and directed four DVDs; and recorded three CDs.

To contact Brienne or to schedule an Eyes Wide Open retreat, conference or seminar, visit the following:

www.briennemurk.com
In Tune Ministries
P.O. Box 1044
St. Charles, IL 60175

For information on Myrrh and In Tune Ministries, visit:
www.myrrh.org

Brienne travels and records with the group *Myrrh*. To order these and other great titles visit: www.myrrh.org

Dreams – A contemporary collection of classic songs of faith, including: When You Believe, Bless the Broken Road, You Raise Me Up, and Only Hope.

Closer – A meditative worship album featuring: Shout to the Lord, I Love You Lord, Ancient of Days, and There is None Like You.

Bridge – This electrifying album is filled with original songs, and compelling spiritual truths that revive both personal faith and spiritual passion.

Myrrh Live – With songs from four of Myrrh's albums, this DVD was recorded live and features the group's awe-inspiring music and transparent testimony.

Be watching for *Eyes Wide Open*— the single—on iTunes!